Maggie Lane's Oriental Patchwork

Books by Maggie Lane

NEEDLEPOINT BY DESIGN

MORE NEEDLEPOINT BY DESIGN

CHINESE RUGS DESIGNED FOR NEEDLEPOINT

RUGS AND WALL HANGINGS

MAGGIE LANE'S NEEDLEPOINT PILLOWS

MAGGIE LANE'S ORIENTAL PATCHWORK

Maggie Lane's
Oriental Patchwork

Maggie Lane

Charles Scribner's Sons   New York

This book is dedicated to Charles Blackburn

Library of Congress Cataloging in Publication Data

Lane, Maggie.
  Maggie Lane's Oriental patchwork.

  Bibliography: p. 104

  1. Patchwork. 2. Clothing and dress. I. Title.
II. Title: Oriental patchwork.
TT835.L33   746.9'2   78-7957
ISBN 0-684-15621-0

1 3 5 7 9 11 13 15 17 19 MD/C 20 18 16 14 12 10 8 6 4 2

Printed in the United States of America

Design by Patricia Smythe

ACKNOWLEDGMENTS

I could never have written this book without the help of these friends:
Charles Blackburn, who designed all the muslin patterns for the costumes in the illustrations;
R. Lans Christensen, who photographed the clothes, the beads, and the earrings;
Lou Arnold and Jerry Brown, who helped me so graciously whenever I selected fabrics for the patchwork;
my husband, Myles, who allowed me to use our living room as a work space and never once complained about the mess;
and Elinor Parker, the book's editor, whose enthusiasm made me very happy.

To every one of these people I give my warmest thanks.

List of Color Illustrations

Contents

How It All Began

For the past year and a half I have been totally absorbed in making the patchwork clothes needed to illustrate this book. The days, weeks, and months I spent on this project have been so full of pleasure that I find it hard to stop sewing. But in order to make it possible for you to profit from my experiences I know I must now park my needle and pick up my pen.

But before I get into the business of giving you instructions on how to create your own patchwork capes and coats, I would like to tell you about the events that led to my interest in patching and my subsequent decision to share with you the discoveries I made in this exciting field of needlework.

The following list of events, though not obviously connected, nevertheless fed into the stream of thought that eventually became this book, *Maggie Lane's Oriental Patchwork*.

In the fall of 1972 I received a letter from Charles Blackburn, then a stranger to me. His purpose in writing was to tell me how very much he had enjoyed my first book (*Needlepoint by Design*). His letter was one of the nicest of its kind that I have ever received. I wrote thanking him for his words of appreciation. Not long afterward I received an invitation to view a collection of his custom-made evening robes and dresses. The show took place in a building on the West Side of New York where Mr. Blackburn designed costumes for Portfolio, the experimental theater that produced *The Fantasticks, I Do, I Do,* and *Philomon*, to name a few of the musicals written by Tom Jones, with music by Harvey Schmidt. (Interesting note: several years earlier Harvey Schmidt had bought from a 57th Street antique shop the very first needlepoint pillow I made for sale, a stag beetle and border all worked in black, brown, gray, and white, later pictured in *Needlepoint by Design*.)

In June of 1973 my husband and I went to Bermuda for our vacation, and when we returned I called Mr. Blackburn because I wanted him to make for me an evening coat out of an antique cashmere shawl I had bought on our trip. I was not brave enough to cut into it, but having seen some of his designs, I knew he could do something beautiful with it. He said he would make the coat for me. We discussed my ideas, and then I invited him to my house for tea.

On the afternoon we had agreed upon, he arrived, I poured, and we sat down, cups and saucers in hand.

Conversation did not begin haltingly. It erupted. We found our interests and attitudes so similar that we talked for over three hours.

When he left, my measurements and the Indian shawl went with him.

A few days later the coat was ready. When I tried it on I was amazed at how cleverly he had used in his design the fabric's plain ivory field and its blue and ivory patterned border. He had in fact been so sure of what he was doing that instead of turning up a hem, he had let the shawl's fringe finish and border the bottom of the coat. And it even fell to exactly the right length!

My admiration for his creative talents then prompted me to ask if he would make a few more things for me.

While writing my first two books I had bought many lengths of beautiful silks and cottons, but had found no time to make them into clothes. And now, with still another book on the way, I knew that for many more months I would be unable to find the time to sew. I really needed someone who would help me bring my wardrobe up to date.

Mr. Blackburn had come into my life at exactly the right time. With a teasing smile he said that he would design and make some clothes for me only if I would promise to stay close to my drafting board, drawing graphs for another book.

Months later, when I had almost finished my first rug book and saw that I might have a little time for sewing, I asked Mr. Blackburn to sell me one of the patterns he had created for me. He agreed to cut me a "muslin."

In all the years that I had been making my own clothes I had never used a muslin pattern. I had always worked with commercial ones made of tissue paper. I had also never made anything designed as simply as Mr. Blackburn's things.

All commercial patterns are full of gussets, gathers, pleats, and darts, every one of them needing intricate and often unintelligible instructions. When following these patterns I found that no sleeves ever went into their armholes properly, necklines never failed to be too tight, and bosom darts always darted in the wrong direction. My friend's patterns need no darts. In each one the crucial fit comes at the shoulders, and from these points the garment flows. The sleeves really fit the armholes, and not one of his necklines ever feels like a hangman's noose.

For the purpose of blocking the large tapestries I had made for my two rug books, I had bought two plywood boards, each measuring 30 by 72 inches, and covered them with muslin. They stood upright against an inner wall of our coat closet. I took them out and placed them side by side on the dining table. I had realized that they would make a simply marvelous cutting board.

Until then I had always used a smaller area, since only the waxed—and hence slippery—dining table had been available. And never before had I used a fabric-covered surface.

On my new cutting boards I spread a length of paisley-printed voile. To my great surprise and pleasure I found I could smooth and straighten the voile and it would stay where I coaxed it, *in place*, ready for cutting.

I took out my newly acquired cloth pattern, laid its five sections on the voile, and was truly delighted to note that the muslin pieces clung to the voile! *I did not need to pin the pattern to the fabric I planned to cut!* What an enormous saving of time!

The beautiful remnant I stood ready to cut was scarcely large enough to make the floating coat I craved. But I discovered that with careful pattern placement there would be *just* enough only if I eliminated all facings and hems and, instead, used bias binding for finishing the edges. So I rushed out immediately and bought a yard of plain voile to match one shade dominant in the paisley print.

On a few occasions in the past I had used bias binding for finishing a dress, but had almost given up the method because in my hands it had hitherto nearly always produced unprofessional-looking results. For one thing, I had never been able to cut any fabric into strips of even width. The fabric always slipped on the table. And then, as a result, the strips were never on the true 45-degree bias angle. Furthermore, before I had heeded Mr. Blackburn's suggestion that I buy a pair of tailor's shears, the scissors I had always used had chewed at fabrics rather than cut them cleanly. But now, with my muslin-covered boards, a pair of shears with razor-sharp blades, a long metal ruler, a triangle, and a white drawing pencil at hand, I found that cutting bias strips need terrify me no more.

In the fall of 1974 I delivered to Charles Scribner's Sons the manuscript for my third book, *Chinese Rugs Designed for Needlepoint*. Then, early in the winter of 1975 the manuscript for *Rugs and Wall Hangings* was put into their hands.

My two years of work had left me quite exhausted. I decided that I would take a brief vacation from needlepoint, for once again I really needed some new clothes, and our apartment was long overdue for some attention and redecorating.

Our bedroom is not large, but I spent several weeks giving it a new look. During the bailing-out that is part of any renovating process I decided to relieve the congestion in my husband's closet. From a tie rack affixed to the inner side of the door, bulging clusters of narrow ties hung in tangled ropes. Unused for years, they seemed ripe for total obscurity, the trash basket I held in my hand. But aware of my husband's New England upbringing, I thought I really ought to ask his permission before I threw anything away. He made it quite clear that he was not yet ready to part with the ties, for he was saving the collection for the day when narrow neckwear would once again be in style. So, reluctantly I left them where they hung and closed the closet door.

Several days later I visited the Scribner Book Store to see what they had most recently added to their very good selection of art books. I picked up a new volume entitled *Japanese Costume and Textile Arts* and leafed through the illustrated pages. Suddenly I was stopped by the picture of a dofuko made for a sixteenth-century Japanese warlord. The robe resembled a kimono, except that instead of crossing in the front and being tied with a belt, it was designed to hang open, uncrossed and unbelted. What riveted my eye, however, was not its cut but its fabric—patchwork, a type I had never seen before. I looked at the picture for several moments while figuring out how the patching was done. Several plain silks of different tones and colors, some small-patterned brocades, and a number of striped fabrics had been cut into squares, rectangles, triangles, parallelograms, and trapezoids, then sewn together in long strips. When these strips were seamed together side by side, they resembled a bird's-eye view of rows and rows of neatly tilled fields (see page 91).

Gathering together the rich and varied fabrics needed to reproduce the effect might present a problem, I thought. Then, like a mirage, the collection of old ties swam enticingly across my mind's eye, a vision seen, so to speak, against lids closed only for the time it takes to blink. The solution to my problem had been given to me.

The Judge and I were to celebrate our seventeenth wedding anniversary in April. That early March day, in the Scribner Book Store, I decided to make and give to my husband as a commemorative present a dofuko like the one illustrated in the volume I held in my hand. I bought the book and took it home.

That evening I told Myles that he really *must* part with his old ties after all, because I had need of them for a project which I assured him would be most worthwhile and as a further bonus would give him real pleasure. I said that I could not tell him just then what I intended to do with them because my plans must be kept secret for the moment. He did not answer me. It may have been because he thought that the irritating subject of his old neckwear had already been fully discussed and the subject closed forever—needing no further comment—or because he knew I could not keep a secret for any length of time at all. He knows me well. Not even a minute went by before I blurted out my reason for wanting his treasured rags. I thrust the book at him, open at the picture of the patchwork dofuko. He peered at it for longer than I thought necessary. When at last he raised his head, he also spoke. "Motion granted. You may *have* the ties," he said grandly.

4

The next morning I gathered them together and put the bundle on the dining table where it made a surprisingly substantial mound.

It was a Saturday, and Myles was at home. I began my work, snipping open the ties, pressing them flat, and preparing them for cutting and patching. More than once my husband left his newspaper in the library and wandered out to see how I was doing. I was amused to note that each time he visited me he would casually poke the pile of ties still intact, caress an old favorite, pick it up, and then try to palm it. Heartlessly I stopped him every time.

The robe took longer to make than I had anticipated because I had to patch each tie into a single piece of a size and shape right for its place in my near duplication of the original patchwork dofuko. But I met the deadline.

When I presented my gift, I saw that it touched and pleased my husband. But soon I also saw that, except as a show piece to be brought out for guests to admire for a minute or two, it would never be worn. The ties, it seemed, were destined never to leave the closet after all. I really didn't mind, however, because I had so enjoyed the actual *process* of making the patchwork robe.

(One day recently I dropped in at my publishers unannounced to see my editor for a moment. When I arrived she was in conference with another executive. But before long they came out of his office, and she introduced him to me. My reputation as tie-snatcher had evidently preceded me. The gentleman advanced toward me, his right hand outstretched to shake mine, but his left one tightly clutching the lower half of the handsome foulard tie he wore. Feigning apprehension, as though anticipating an assault on his neckwear, he said, "I understand that you walk around with a pair of scissors handy and lop off the ends of all ties you admire.")

Once I had finished my work on the apartment, I turned my attention to sewing for myself. That summer I made quite a few simple, floating coats and bias slip dresses to wear under them. By then I had come to one conclusion: that a fabric's texture, color, and surface pattern, if any, are very important when it comes to creating a "look." But I had reached more than a conclusion—I had reached a *conviction* about the cut of a garment: *good cut* is the most *vital* requirement, the very essence, so to speak, of a "look." To me, cut represents the *bones* of a good design upon which fabric becomes the *flesh*.

While making my summer ensembles, it bothered me not at all to use the same two muslins over and over again, for their cut fitted and pleased me. A friend once asked me if I did not feel that I was always wearing the same costume. I replied that the design for a Chinese chiang-sam has remained relatively unchanged for years, and the way a Japanese kimono is made is still the same as it has been for centuries. Garments made without a single variation in cut but of differing colors and fabrics all seem unique to me.

My collection of clothes kept growing until it reached the stage where the things in it became interchangeable. Depending on my mood I could mix or match the colors of floating coats and bias slip dresses, all of whose edges, incidentally, were neatly finished with narrow bias binding.

The actual *making* of these simple, fluid things gave me real pleasure. No problems or doubts as to fit ever troubled me because I knew that each garment would hang just the way it should. I kept sewing until late summer. By then I had several bags bulging with scraps saved, for what I did not as yet know.

Then, without any warning, the first crisp day of autumn blew in, and I realized that I must make a light street-length cape to wear over my all-season wardrobe. I already owned a Blackburn muslin for a floor-length cape, cut in almost a full circle. I had used it once, having made it in wool paisley, and it had been most successful.

The pattern for the cape had required a very wide fabric. So I knew I must look for another handsome piece of cloth in a wide width, for a narrow one would need to be pieced. Pieced? Suddenly I remembered all the pieces— the scraps saved from my summer sewing craze. Why not use them to make the cape in the Japanese style of patchwork I had used for the dofuko? I could quilt it with something light and warm, line it, and finish it with bias binding.

I plunged into the project with great excitement, because the fun of patching and its aesthetic rewards would give me pleasure for a long time. Making patchwork was faster and easier this time because I did not have to piece each patch before putting it in its place in a strip.

Soon I had finished the cape, then looking at it objectively realized that I might need a special kind of courage to wear it, for it was, after all, somewhat bizarre—nothing like it had ever before been seen around these parts. Even in Japan its kind has probably not been worn since the sixteenth century. There is, however, a bit of the actor in every one of us. That is why I like to call my clothes "costumes."

So I tried on one of my bias slip dresses with a floating coat over it, then put on the cape. I liked the effect. I tried another dress and coat under the cape, then another. I was delighted to see that there were endless combinations possible in this kind of dressing in layers. Each dress or coat I put on to wear with the patchwork went well with it because scraps of all the dress and coat fabrics had been used in making the cape. I also found that the cape went with many colors of shoes, bags, and gloves.

This proved to me that patchwork is remarkably versatile. I found later that it is also practical. Spots or stains are hardly discernible on its piebald surface, and if it wrinkles, it does not seem to matter, since patchwork, by its very nature, is already crazed, and when quilted wrinkles hardly at all. (Furthermore, good, light quilting is very warm.) But best of all, making patchwork things encourages creativity by offering its maker an opportunity to express his or her own very personal taste in design and color harmony.

My cape elicited no notice the first time I wore it. Emboldened, I wore it a second time, almost casually. One or two people did comment on it. The third time I put it on I went out with few qualms, even with some assurance. More people spoke to me about it. And thereafter, whenever I wore it, strangers would stop me on the streets to tell me they thought my cape a work of art. So finally I wore it with pride.

The winter of 1976–77 broke several records. *It was cold*! I hastened to add another layer to my costume, a quilted patchwork tabard to go with the cape —to be worn under it, but over the dress and floating coat.

Then I decided to make a *really* warm outer coat. Once again I had a conference with my friend Charles. His solution to my description of the coat I wanted was the muslin for the "Magyar" coat, the pattern I consider the most unique of all his designs. I made it in unpatched but quilted fabric and was so pleased with it that I made it again, this time in the wintry black and white patchwork seen in Plates 7 and 8. I quilted it with two layers of fluffy woolen interlining. When it was finished it was still light, but *it was warm!*

By this time my friends were telling me that I should write a book about patchwork. The idea appealed to me for two reasons: I could then go on patching without any sense of guilt, and of course my wardrobe would be even further enhanced, since I could make all samples in my own size.

But a book on patchwork clothes needed patterns. I did not own as many muslins as I felt a book should offer. So once again I called on Charles for help. I had already found his designs practical and easy to make and wear. But most important to me, I found them beautiful. His ability to design clothes with few seams and without darts would enable the patcher to create costumes made up of only a few flat, untormented pieces of patchwork.

Charles and I saw eye to eye when it came to returning to the basics of design. The kind of clothing that had for centuries been worn in the Orient became our source of inspiration. The resulting collection of twelve designs for men's and women's clothing includes patterns for coats, capes, jackets, dresses, skirts, and Indian pants and is offered in the following pages. With each pattern a few directions are given. You will also find instructions on how to make five types of patchwork of oriental cast.

Of course you may use unpatched fabric to make clothes from the patterns in this book, or you may make patchwork clothing following the directions and outlines of commercial paper patterns. The decision is yours.

My only hope is that you will enjoy this book and that it will help you to patch with pleasure, not pain.

The Advantages of Patchwork

In the previous chapter I mentioned several of patchwork's praiseworthy properties: it hardly shows spots, stains, or wrinkles; it goes with many colors of accessories; and it offers its creator a rewarding way to express his or her taste in color harmony and design. I might add that patchwork, because it encourages the sewer to use material that would otherwise be thrown away, meets our present vital need to conserve rather than to waste.

As a further asset, patchwork can become a fabric into which valued memorabilia may be worked with ease. Handsome pieces of antique lace, a cherished christening robe folded away in tissue paper now yellow with age, a baby's old bib, fragile remnants of embroidery (which can be strengthened by backing with a support of new fabric)—all these treasures may be stored away somewhere in your home, just waiting to be resurrected and given a new life. They would add a *most* personal touch to your patchwork.

Fabrics that do not seem to fit into your color scheme can be coaxed into place by a dye bath. Rit and Tintex offer a range of colors that can be used for tinting or dyeing both plain and printed fabrics as well as laces and embroideries. You need not worry about uneven coloring because the pieces you will use in patching are never large enough for such variations to matter.

A final fillip to a piece of patchwork could be a bit of needlepoint made expressly for its place in the design. A signature, a monogram, or a cryptic cipher worked on very fine canvas might turn your patchwork into what could become a signed heirloom of great value.

Necessary Equipment

Sewing patchwork clothes can be an easy and pleasant pastime if you have the right equipment. I have found that the following things are really essential to the serious sewer, and most of them are needed by the patchwork maker.

A big table or other high surface   The area must be big because it will be used for cutting muslin patterns, cutting the fabrics out of which you will make your clothes, or holding all the piles of scraps you will be using when patching. I recommend two pieces of plywood 30 by 72 inches, covered with unbleached muslin. This fabric can be stretched across the surface of each board, folded around the edges, and stapled to the back of the board. Cover the staples with strips of masking tape or twill tape. Otherwise the staples will scratch the surface upon which you lay your boards. Or you can lay a protective cover over your table before you put the boards on it. When not in use the boards can easily be stored in a closet.

Good scissors   Wiss makes the kind I use, inlaid dressmaker's shears, no. 29, 9 inches long, with black handles. They also make the shears 8 inches long if you want a smaller pair. Sharp scissors are *essential* to the sewer, but even more to the patcher, since only patches with clean-cut, straight edges can be precisely joined to produce a neat piece of patchwork.

A long metal ruler   Mine is 45 inches long and 1½ inches wide. It is made by Fairgate; *120-A* is printed on it. It is essential for outlining bias strips and for use in outlining patterns on muslin.

A right-angle triangle   Mine is see-through plastic, 10 by 10 by 14 inches. This tool is essential for the 45-degree angle you will want to find easily when you cut bias strips. Place one side of the triangle along the edge of the table, then, on the table, lay your ruler against the hypotenuse of the triangle and you will have a true 45-degree guide for marking and cutting bias strips.

A turner   This tool is for turning folded and stitched bias strips right side out to make spaghetti straps or belts.

An indelible marking pen, a colored pencil, or a white one, for outlining bias strips and other markings.

A steam iron and holder.

An ironing board with a clean, well-padded surface.

A spray bottle Mine is plastic with a squeeze handle, the kind you can buy for misting plants. I use it for dampening fabrics when I press them straight, in preparation for cutting. I also use it when I press seams open. I spray a mist of real moisture on an already open seam, then re-press the seam to make it *stay* open.

Ball-point pins These are essential when pinning together silk fabrics and for use on all sheers.

A sewing machine, unless you sew very fast by hand!

Ball-point needles for the sewing machine. They will make sewing on silks and sheers a pleasure, since they do not cause fabrics to pucker along the seams.

Cotton thread, or silk if you prefer.

A thimble.

A pincushion.

A pair of tiny snipping scissors, for opening seams when you have made a mistake.

Pattern Making

The patterns in this book are presented as drawings on graph paper. They have been reduced to fit a book-size page. Nevertheless, in each drawing a large graph square still represents a square inch. Several ways of restoring the drawings to their original size are suggested here.

Lay a piece of pressed, unbleached muslin on a large, flat surface. Secure the edges of the cloth with pins or anything handy to keep it in place. Use a felt-tipped pen and a T square. Draw horizontal lines on the muslin. Separate each line from the next line by the width of an inch. Draw vertical lines in the same manner, separating each line from the next line by the width of an inch. The resulting grid will outline squares, each of which will measure one square inch. On this grid you can restore to full size any pattern in this book by carefully following the reduced drawing. As I said before, in the reduced drawings each square in the grid represents one square inch.

You may prefer to buy large sheets of graph paper and tape them together, then draw the full-scale pattern on this ready-made grid.

If large sheets of graph paper are not available you may prefer to draw the grid on brown wrapping paper. Follow the instructions given previously for drawing the grid on muslin.

You can use the paper pattern as a cutting guide for the pieces of fabric you will cut to make your clothes, but I would strongly recommend that you give up paper patterns and use muslins instead.

The advantages of muslins are many:

You can baste together pieces of a muslin pattern, try on the resulting sample garment, and make on it any necessary corrections that will make it fit you exactly.

You can add extra width where necessary simply by sewing additional strips of muslin to the original piece, drawing fit-correction lines on this added strip, and then cutting off any excess muslin.

Muslin pattern pieces need not be pinned to the fabric you will cut to make your clothes. Muslin will not creep on your fabric; neither will it float away in the slightest breeze as tissue patterns will.

Muslin patterns, unlike paper patterns, do not become brittle with age, so they last indefinitely. They do not tear easily, and their corners do not wear out as a result of constant pinning.

When not in use muslins can be folded and neatly stored in marked envelopes about 11 by 14 inches.

Sewing Methods

This chapter covers subjects related to sewing. Most of the hints that follow apply to making patched or unpatched clothes.

Preparing Your Fabric for Cutting

Cottons and linens Preshrink all cottons and linens. Wet them thoroughly in a tub of water. Hang them up to dry. Steam and press them carefully, making sure that the warp and the woof—the horizontal and vertical threads —are at right angles to each other. Many fabrics are sold whose warp and woof threads are *not* at right angles to each other. Such fabrics, if cut without correcting this fault, will *never* hang correctly.

Tip If your fabric is too stiff for your purposes, you can soften it somewhat by pouring a good splash of fabric softener into the tub of water used for preshrinking. Leave the fabric in this bath for a while. When you take the fabric out of the tub, *do not rinse it*. Leave the softener in the fabric.

Silks Silks usually need little preparation, since they are, as a rule, more carefully woven than the cheaper cottons, and the warp and woof threads are usually at right angles to each other.

Wools Preshrink all wools. This can be done by spraying the wool with a light mist of water. Cover the misted wool with a piece of clean cotton fabric. Press the cotton-covered wool lightly so as not to produce any shine or pressure marks on the woolen fabric.

Synthetic fabrics Rayons, nylons, Dacrons, and other synthetics are fabrics I prefer not to use, since I find the natural fibers more comfortable to wear. Natural fibers also feel better in the hand and seem to hang more naturally on the body. Furthermore, since most of the costumes in this book have been inspired by styles of long ago when there *were* no synthetics, I have in every case used only fabrics made with natural fibers.

Make sure that the fabric lies straight and flat on your cutting surface. **Cutting**
Always tear a strip off the end of a length of fabric before placing it on the **the Fabric**
cutting board. Lay the torn end of the fabric along one end of the cutting
board, and one selvage side of the fabric along one side of the cutting board.
In this way you can make sure that the warp and the woof threads will be at
right angles to each other.

Lay your muslin pattern pieces on the fabric, making sure that the pattern
pieces are also lined up properly with the lengthwise grain of the fabric.

Cut the fabric with good, sharp shears that have long blades. Do not nibble
and snip at the fabric. Use most of the length of the blades for each incision
you make in the fabric.

Always stay-stitch—by machine—every bias or curved edge of a fabric **Stay-stitching**
pattern piece cut ready for use in a garment. Stay-stitches should be sewn **and**
³⁄₈ inch to ½ inch away from the edge of the fabric. Often a double row of **Directional**
stitching is advisable. The purpose of stay-stitching is to keep the edges of the **Stitching**
fabric pattern piece from stretching. It is particularly important to stay-stitch
neckline edges. Sew the shoulder seams first, from neck to shoulder. (This is
directional stitching—from the wider to the narrower part of the cut fabric.)
Then stay-stitch the left side of the neckline, from the bottom of the V neck in
front, up to the shoulder seam, then around to the center back. Repeat this
process on the right side. I always use two rows of stay-stitching at the neckline. At the beginning and the ending of each row of stitching, I secure the
thread by sewing a reverse stitch or two.

Sew side seams on the A-line dresses and coats from the bottom to the top.
This is directional stitching—from the wider to the narrower part of the
fabric. Sew all bell sleeves and flared sleeves from bottom to top. This too is
directional stitching.

All the patterns in this book allow for a ⁵⁄₈-inch seam wherever the pattern
pieces will be joined together. (Each of these seams is indicated on the small-
scale drawings by a row of dotted lines.) I have, however, given no seam
allowance where a hem or a facing is usually used. This is because I recommend the use of bias bindings for all finished edges. But if you prefer to hem
and face your finished edges, add a ⁵⁄₈-inch seam allowance to your muslin
pattern wherever you will need it. And also add the width of any hem you
would like to turn up.

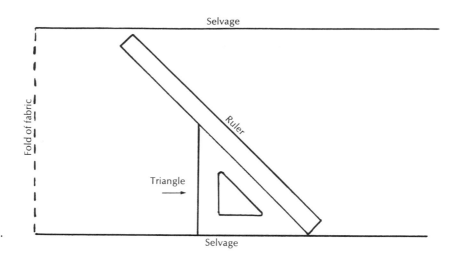

Finding the true bias.

Bias Binding

Bias binding eliminates the bulk of hems and facings. It can be made of the same fabric as the garment on which it will be sewn, or it can be of a contrasting color or tone.

On your cutting boards lay the fabric you intend to use for bias binding. Make sure that the horizontal and vertical threads of the fabric lie parallel to the ends and sides of your cutting surface. Place one side of a right-angle triangle (10 by 10 by 14 inches is the size I use) along the edge of the cutting board. Take a long metal ruler (45 by 1½ inches is the size I use) and lay it on the table with one side of it against the hypotenuse of the triangle. The ruler will then lie at a 45-degree angle to the edge of the table. Use a colored or white pencil, or an indelible marking pen, to draw a line along one side of the ruler. Draw another line along the other side of the ruler. Then move the ruler so that one side of it lies along one of the lines you have already drawn, and draw a line along the other side of the ruler. Continue drawing parallel diagonal lines on the fabric. The spaces between the ruled lines will be the width of your ruler, that is, 1½ inches wide.

Cut along the diagonal lines you have drawn on the fabric, and you will have bias strips 1½ inches in width. Sew these strips together, right sides face to face, and straight ends of the strips meeting as shown in the diagram. Press all seams open and cut off the little ears of excess fabric.

The width of any bias strip should be four times the width it will be when turned and finished, plus an additional ¼ inch. This extra ¼ inch seems to get lost when the bias binding, after being machine stitched to the garment, is folded ready for the hand stitching needed to hold it in place.

For bias strips wider or narrower than your ruler's width, you must measure the required widths and mark them, using the first 45-degree diagonal line you have drawn as your guideline. Make width marks away from both the top and the bottom of this diagonal guideline, holding your measuring ruler at right angles to it. Then lay your long ruler parallel to the original diagonal guideline and draw lines between the width-mark lines at the top and bottom of the original guideline.

When preparing to bind the edges of your garment, lay it flat on the table, right side of the fabric up. Lay the bias binding, right side down, on the gar-

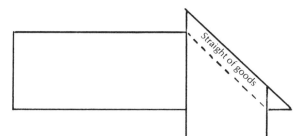

Joining bias seam binding strips. Lay right sides together and sew on straight of goods.

ment. The binding must be placed so that one edge of it follows the edge of the garment. Handle the bias ribbon with care, as though you were handling ribbons of very short, tender piecrust, or lengths of soft noodles. In this way you will not stretch the bias ribbon. Pin the bias strip to the garment every inch or so. Where bias binding goes around the outer edge of a curve, ease the binding by widening it. To do this, take the two sides of the bias strip and pull each side outward from the center of the strip. When the bias binding goes around the inner edge of a curve, for instance, at the neckline, stretch the binding slightly. On all curves, pin the bias binding to the garment every ¼ inch. Pin at right angles to the edges of the binding and the garment. When you machine stitch the binding to the garment, the machine's needle will jump right over the pins.

With very slippery or fragile fabrics you may make the cutting and handling of bias strips much easier if you lay lengths of narrow magic tape on the strips marked on the fabric *before* you cut the fabric into bias strips. Leave the magic tape on the bias strips after you have cut them. However, remove the magic tape from the ends of the bias strips. Here you will have to sew the bias strips together, and then press the seams open. Magic tape is hard to pull off the bias strip if pressed on it. And a sewing machine needle will become sticky if forced to sew over magic tape. You must also remove the magic tape from any places where the bias tape has to be stretched or eased. Remove the remaining magic tape from the bias binding after the binding has been machine stitched to the garment.

Machine stitch 1½-inch-wide bias binding ⅜ inch away from its edge and the edge of the garment. Then fold back and press the binding so that its wider part covers the edge of the garment. Then, holding the garment with its inside facing you, fold the bias binding toward you so that its free edge meets its other edge and the garment's edge. Then fold the bias strip toward you again so that the first fold in the bias binding meets the line of machine stitching that joins the bias binding to the garment. Pin the folded binding in place, then, by hand, sew its folded edge to the machine-stitched seam. Use invisible stitches. (I am still trying to invent one. The slip stitch is as close as I can come.) Just make sure that the thread you use for this last step matches the binding! Press the bound edge lightly after you have finished sewing it.

(*Note*: When I begin to pin a bias binding to a garment, I turn toward me and fold back ¼ inch of binding at the place where I start pinning. This eliminates a raw edge. When the binding has been pinned all the way around the edges of the garment and reaches the finish line—which is also the place where the bias binding began—I let the end of the binding overlap the fold at the beginning of the binding. This becomes an almost invisible joining and can later be tacked into place if you so desire.)

15

**Finishing Seams
Inside a Garment**
Use bias binding to cover the raw edges of all armhole seams. Cut off part of the ⅝-inch seam allowance in the armhole, leaving about ¼ to ⅓ inch. Then bind this newly cut, neat edge.

For all side seams in sheer garments, either use French seams or press seams open and fold under the raw edges. Then, by hand, stitch the resulting edge, the fold, to the garment, using invisible stitches.

French seams With *right* sides of the fabric out, machine stitch a seam only ¼ inch from the edges of the pieces to be joined. Press the seam open. Then fold together the two pieces thus joined so that the *insides* of the garment are facing out and the raw edges parallel to the narrow seam lie between the *right* sides of the two joined pieces of the garment. Then machine stitch another seam ⅜ inch away from the edge of the folded and pressed first seam. The second seam will trap the raw edges next to the original seam.

Unquilted Patchwork

All the patchwork summer coats illustrated in this book have been under-lined rather than lined; that is, each piece of patchwork has been placed, right side up, on a piece of voile and hand basted to it before being cut into a shape to be used in making the garment. Smooth the patchwork out, flat, on the voile, and pin the two layers together, pins at right angles to the patch-work seams. Use invisible basting stitches to attach the patchwork to the voile. Sew along the pressed-open seams of the patchwork. This process will *keep* all the patchwork seams open. Only after a piece of patchwork has been thus mounted should you lay the muslin pattern on it and cut the patchwork.

Finish the insides of each garment with bias tape: cut off excess seam al-lowance in the armholes, leaving only ¼ inch, and then bind. For the side seams, trim away excess, then lay and pin a piece of bias tape over the open seam. Turn under the raw edges of the bias tape and catch the folded edges to the voile underlining. Finish all edges that show with bias binding.

Quilted Patchwork

Quilting is the process of joining together two layers of fabric with a third layer of warmth-giving material between them, like making a woolen-filled sandwich. The three layers must then be sewn together in order to keep the warmth-giving layer from creeping or stretching. There are many ways of sewing these layers together. In every garment illustrated in this book, however, I have used the channel stitching method: by hand, sew—with basting stitches—along the seams joining the patches together (see preceding chapter).

Always quilt each piece of the garment before machine stitching the pieces together to make the garment.

Line all quilted garments with a separate layer of fabric, preferably silk, to conceal all raw seams. Sew the quilted garment to the lining along the side and shoulder seams, and baste together the raw edges of the quilted coat and the lining, ready for binding. On all quilted things, use ½-inch finished binding. Cut this bias binding 2¼ inches wide.

For the warmth-giving layer of quilted clothing, use any lightweight fluffy woolen material made expressly for the purpose. If you want something really light and warm, use mohair fabric. It is expensive but could be worth the extra money it costs.

Patterns for Garments

The patterns in this book have been designed so simply—with no darts, facings, or hems—that instructions are really superfluous. In fact, the experienced sewer will be amazed at how little time it will take to make the bias slip dress or blouse, the basic unlined coat, or a pair of Indian pants. The novice, however, should have the benefit of some helpful hints on how to go about making the garments. Therefore a few guidelines accompany the pattern for each article of clothing.

The sizes indicated are as follows:

Petite	Sizes 4 to 6
Small	Sizes 8 to 10
Medium	Sizes 12 to 14
Large	Sizes 16 to 18

The straight of goods is always parallel to the grid lines on the graphs, except as indicated on the graphs for the Magyar coat scarf.

BASIC COAT

THREE PIECES
Front cut two
Back cut one
Sleeve cut two

Patterns for a bell sleeve and for a sleeve with a semicircular flounce have also been included here. The flounced sleeve is *not* good for patchwork. It is good for the soft cottons, silks, and linens that hang well on the bias. To make a double flounce, make two pattern pieces for the flounce, one that is one inch shorter than the other. See the dotted line on the pattern.

The basic coat pattern can be used as a jacket pattern or a floor-length evening coat pattern in addition to the street length given here. Simply shorten or lengthen at the hem line.

Front   Lay center front of pattern along selvage, or lengthwise grain of fabric. Cut right and left front pieces.

Back   Lay center back of pattern along lengthwise fold of fabric and cut one piece, or add ⅝-inch seam allowance to pattern at center back, and cut two pieces, left back and right back.

Sleeve   Lay center of sleeve pattern along the lengthwise grain of fabric and cut right and left sleeves.

Sew shoulder and side seams. Press seams open. Sew sleeve seams. Press seams open. Sew sleeves to coat. The following detailed instructions may be helpful to those who find it difficult to sew the armhole seam:

Turn the coat *inside out*. The sleeve must be *right side out*. Hold the edges of the sleeve and the armhole of the coat together. Match and pin at underarm seams, at shoulder seam, and at top center of sleeve, and match and pin where single points are cut on sleeve and coat front and double points are cut on sleeve and coat back. Pin on the coat side, running the pins at right angles to what will be your armhole seam. Pin so that the pins point toward the armhole, away from the coat. Hold the edges of the coat and sleeve in your left hand. Pin with the right hand. Run the pins through the fabric two or three times as you would if using a sewing needle to make two or three stitches. Pin every ½ inch along the seam line, or even every ¼ inch if you like. Ease the coat armhole to fit the sleeve at the underarm, and ease the cap of the sleeve to fit the coat armhole—from the single point in front across the shoulder to the double point in back. *I repeat: Pin on the coat side of the armhole. Machine stitch on the sleeve side of the armhole.*

The machine needle will jump right over the pins, all of which have been run in at *right angles* to the seam line.

Finish the raw edges of the coat and sleeves with bias binding.

The basic coat looks very good if slit open at the side seams—up to the widest part of the hip. If you want to make it this way, cut the pattern with straight edges where the slits will be.

See the basic coats in Plates 2–6, 9, 12–13, and 16–18.

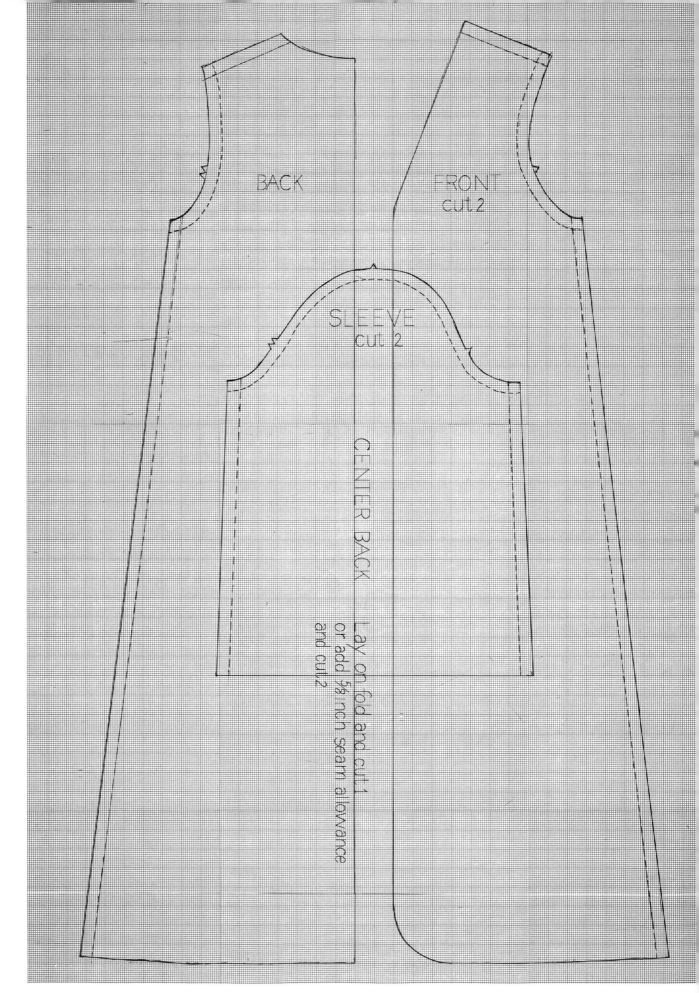

BACK

FRONT
cut 2

SLEEVE
cut 2

CENTER BACK Lay on fold and cut 1
or add ⅝ inch seam allowance
and cut 2

BASIC COAT—PETITE

Plate 3 Front of basic coat, made of black and white cotton fabrics worked in the manner of sixteenth-century Japanese patchwork. (See page 20.)

Plate 4 Front of basic coat made of bone and white cotton textured and openwork fabrics worked in fish-scale patchwork. (See page 20.)

Plate 5 Front of basic coat made of black, brown, and gray cotton fabrics worked in arrowhead patchwork. (See page 20.)

Plate 6 Back of basic coat made of black and red cotton fabrics worked in the manner of sixteenth-century Japanese patchwork. (See page 20.)

Plate 7   Back of Magyar coat shown in Plate 8.
(See page 31.)

Plate 8 Front of Magyar coat made of black, tan, and bone fabrics—silk, wool, and cotton—interlined and quilted. The hand stitching is sewn along the vertical seams. Worked in the manner of sixteenth-century Japanese patchwork. (See page 31.)

Plate 9 Front of short basic coat made of brown and black cotton voile patched to reproduce a pattern found in an old Japanese needlework sampler. Sleeveless bias overblouse and Indian pants complete the outfit. (See page 20.)

Plate 10 Front of evening dress with sleeveless bias blouse top supporting long gathered skirt made of mauve, blue, navy, and magenta cotton fabrics worked in the manner of sixteenth-century Japanese patchwork. Triangular "sleeves," sewn to the sleeveless bias blouse only across the shoulders, end in fabric tassels. (See page 40.)

Plate 11 Front of kite made of celadon cotton voile with blue and celadon printed cotton voile appliquéd in circular patches at shoulders, wrists, and at center front, and worn over an evening dress: sleeveless bias blouse top joined to long skirt made with narrow vertical strips of printed cotton voile. (See page 64.)

Plate 12 Back of unfinished short basic coat made of eggplant, russet and green, gold, silver, and bone, and several printed fabrics worked in patchwork designed to simulate a typical pattern found in Japanese Imari porcelain. (See page 20.)

Plate 13 Front of short basic coat made of eggplant, russet and green, gold, silver, and bone, and several printed fabrics, worked in patchwork designed to simulate a typical pattern found in Japanese Imari porcelain. Shown with tan silk overblouse and eggplant silk Indian pants. (See page 20.)

Plate 14 Front of man's karate jacket made of blue and white cotton batik and madras, worked in patchwork designed to simulate a typical pattern found in Japanese Imari porcelain. (See page 69.)

Plate 15 Man's or woman's kangaroo shirt made of heavy raw silk fabrics of natural tones worked in arrowhead patchwork. Shown with a turtleneck sweater and tan silk Indian pants. (See page 83.)

Plate 16 Front of basic coat made of orange, yellow, and bone cotton and silk fabrics and old embroideries worked in the manner of sixteenth-century Japanese patchwork. Sleeveless bias overblouse and Indian pants underneath. (See page 20.)

Plate 17 Front view of two basic coats worn with sleeveless bias overblouses and Indian pants. The navy and bone printed silk coat is slit up the sides and has sleeves with a double flounce. The burnt orange Indian gauze coat has circular lace pieces appliquéd on it. The gauze behind each appliquéd lace circle has been cut away. This coat, too, has been slit up the sides. It has bell sleeves. (See page 20.)

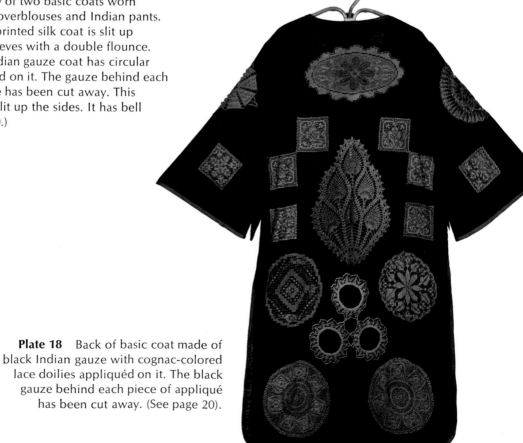

Plate 18 Back of basic coat made of black Indian gauze with cognac-colored lace doilies appliquéd on it. The black gauze behind each piece of appliqué has been cut away. (See page 20).

Plate 19   Front of Magyar coat made of rust, beige, and black cotton paisley, interlined and quilted. The hand stitching following the paisley design. (See page 31.)

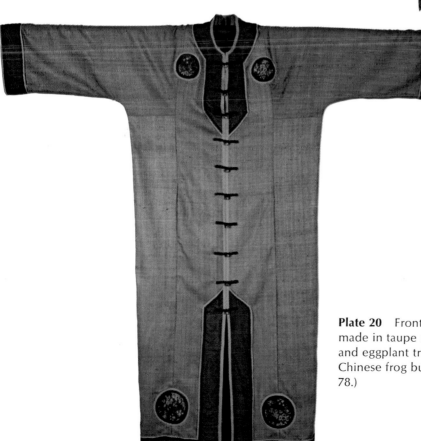

Plate 20   Front of man's caftan made in taupe raw silk with russet and eggplant trim and appliqué. Chinese frog buttons. (See page 78.)

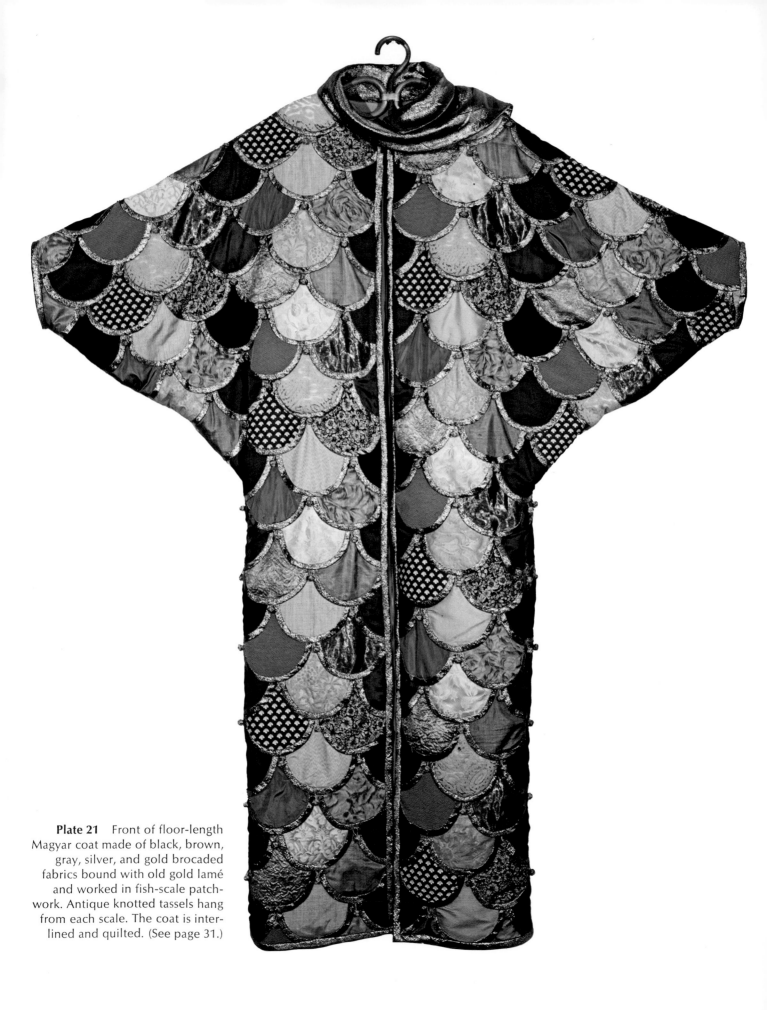

Plate 21 Front of floor-length Magyar coat made of black, brown, gray, silver, and gold brocaded fabrics bound with old gold lamé and worked in fish-scale patchwork. Antique knotted tassels hang from each scale. The coat is interlined and quilted. (See page 31.)

Plate 22 Front of street-length cape made in blue, green, and bone fabrics and embroideries —silk, wool, and cotton—worked in the manner of sixteenth-century Japanese patchwork. (See page 51.)

Plate 23 (Right) Long pendant necklaces for wearing with patchwork. The beads, on silken cord, are strung in the Chinese manner with spaces between them. (See page 102.)

Plate 24 (Below) Earrings to wear with patchwork. Any bead with a small post through it ending in a loop at the top of it can be hung on the curved wire that goes through the pierced ear lobe. (See page 102.)

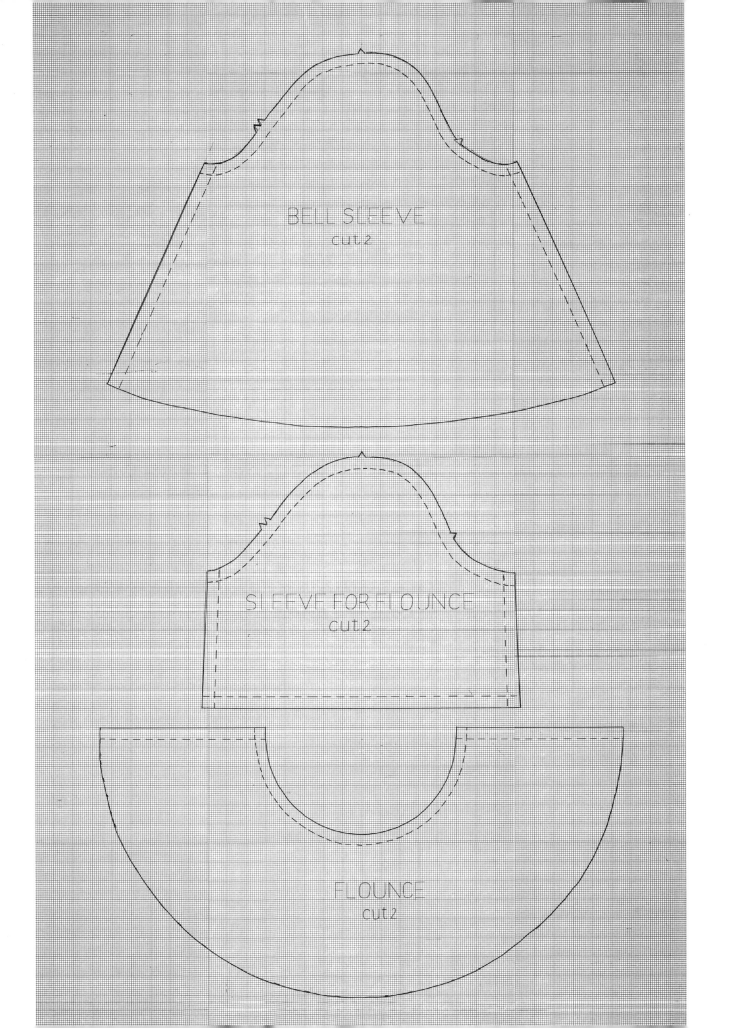

BELL SLEEVE
cut 2

SLEEVE FOR FLOUNCE
cut 2

FLOUNCE
cut 2

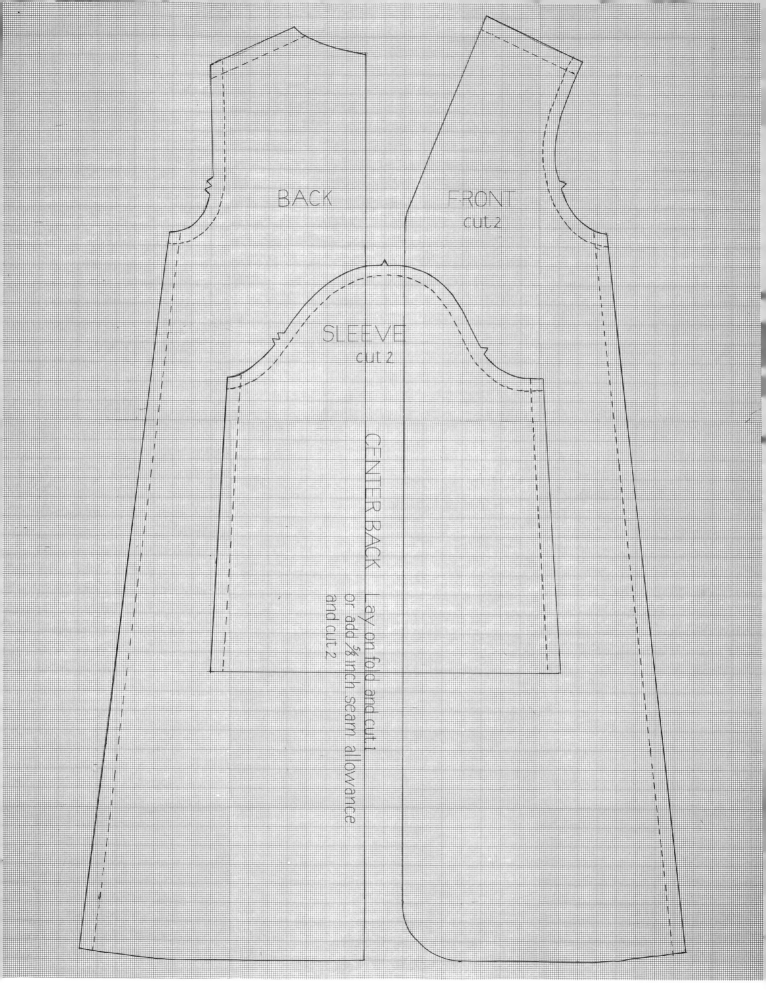

BACK

FRONT
cut 2

SLEEVE
cut 2

CENTER BACK   Lay on fold and cut 1
or add ⅝ inch seam allowance
and cut 2

BASIC COAT—MEDIUM

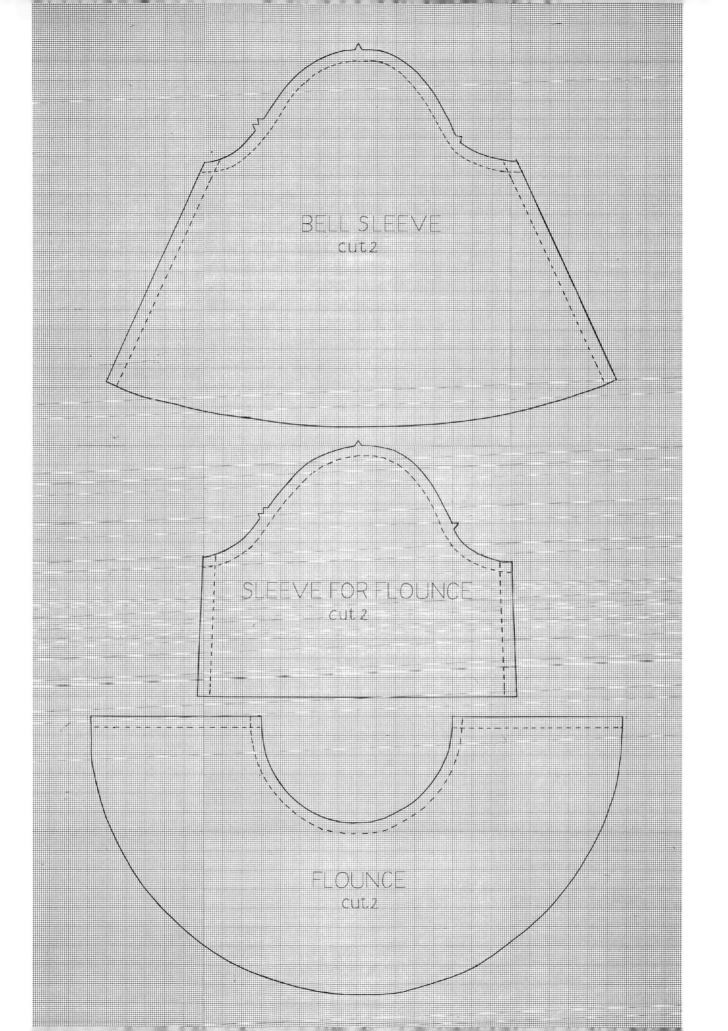

BELL SLEEVE
cut 2

SLEEVE FOR FLOUNCE
cut 2

FLOUNCE
cut 2

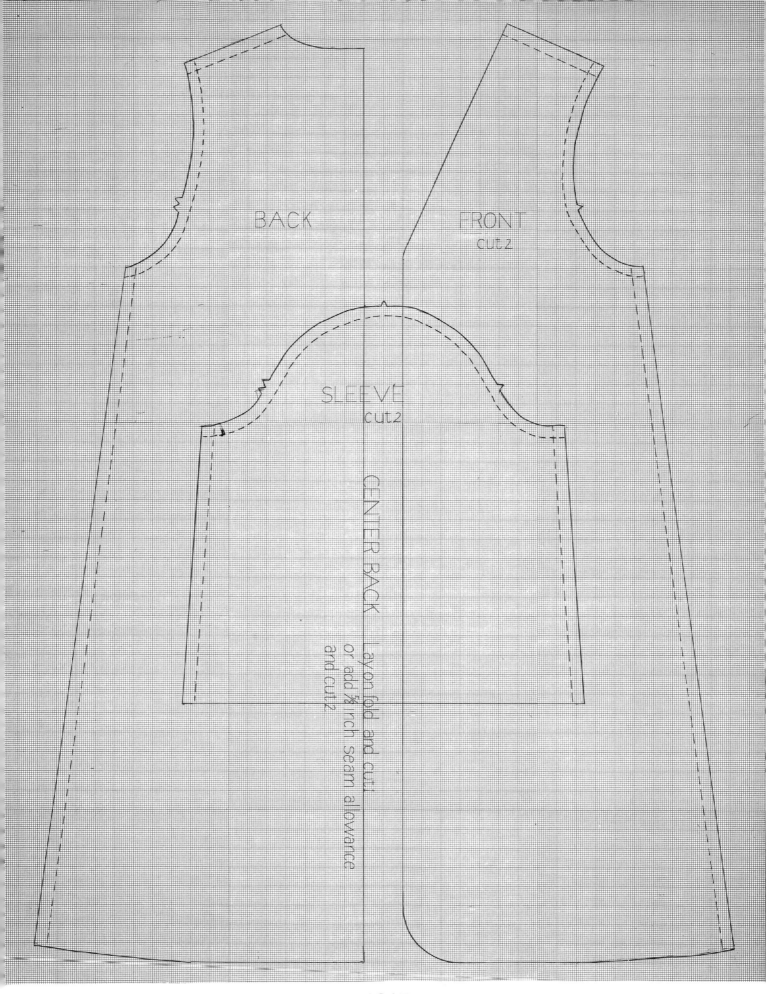

BACK

FRONT
cut 2

SLEEVE
cut 2

CENTER BACK   Lay on fold and cut,
or add ⅝ inch seam allowance
and cut 2

BASIC COAT—LARGE

BELL SLEEVE
cut 2

SLEEVE FOR FLOUNCE
cut 2

FLOUNCE
cut 2

MAGYAR COAT

FOUR PIECES
Front   cut two
Back   cut one
Sleeve   cut four
Scarf   cut one

Sew sleeve pieces to front and back pieces from A to B. Press seams open. Sew shoulder seams, from neck edge to wrist. Sew underarm and side seams, all one seam, from wrist to break at underarm, then down the sides. Clip seam allowance at underarm.

Make a lining like the coat and baste it to the coat. Finish the lined coat with bias binding around all edges of the coat except at the neck.

With right sides together, sew one neck edge of the scarf to the neck edge of the coat, from left side around center back to right side. Clip seam allowance of coat neckline. Fold scarf inside out down its lengthwise center line. Stitch around scarf from right neckline down to and around the double points at the end of the scarf. Trim and clip seam allowance on scarf. Turn scarf right side out and slip stitch free side of scarf neckline to coat neckline.

Use fur hooks and eyes to join the center front of the coat, or use decorative but functional frogs.

See Plates 7, 8, 19, and 21.

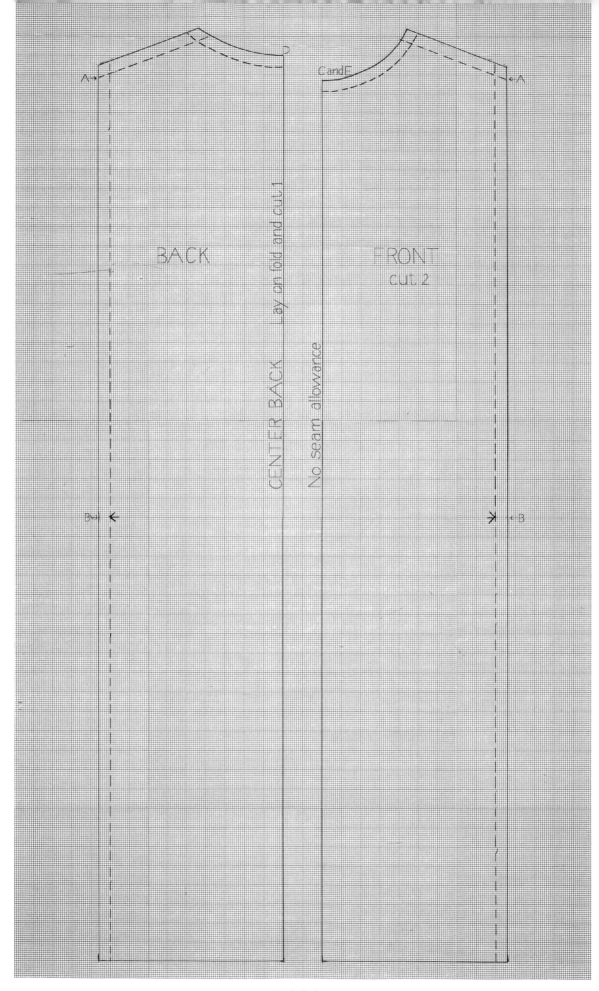

A→   C and F   A

BACK   CENTER BACK   Lay on fold and cut 1   FRONT
cut 2

No seam allowance

B→ ←   ← →   ← B

MAGYAR COAT—PETITE

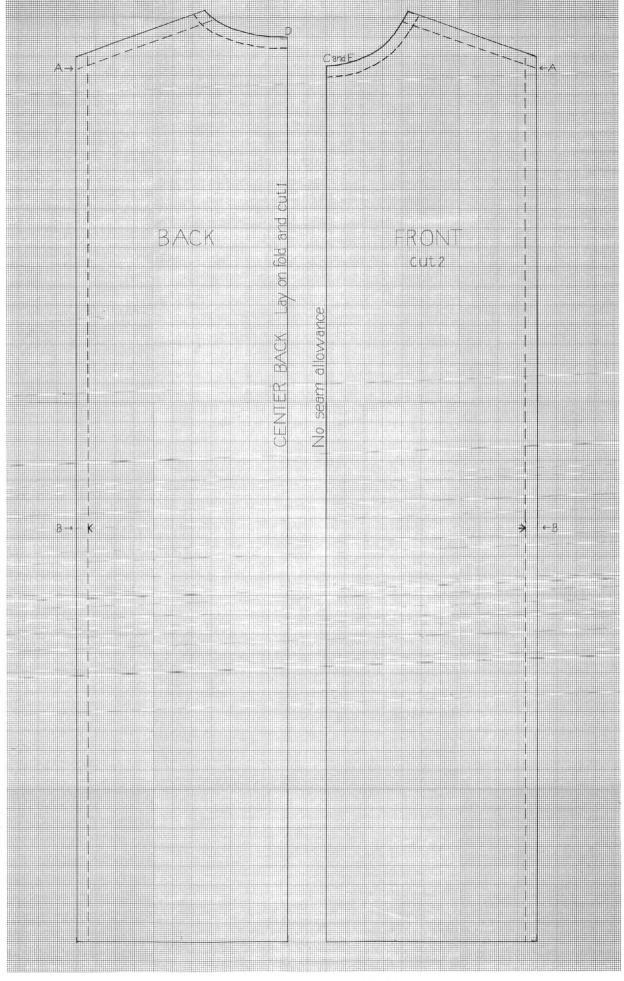

MAGYAR COAT—SMALL

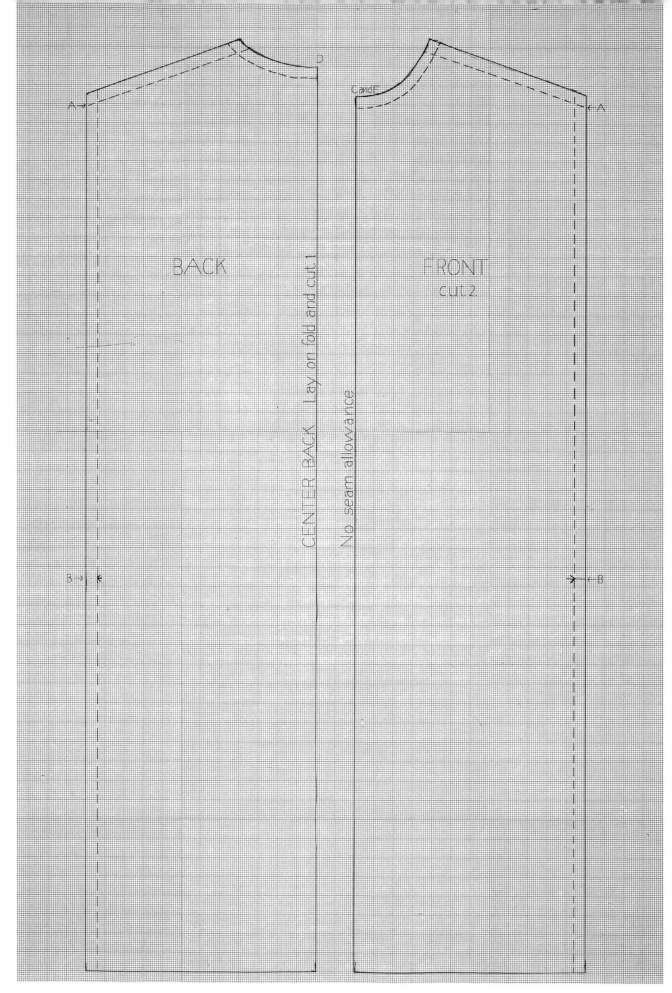

MAGYAR COAT—MEDIUM

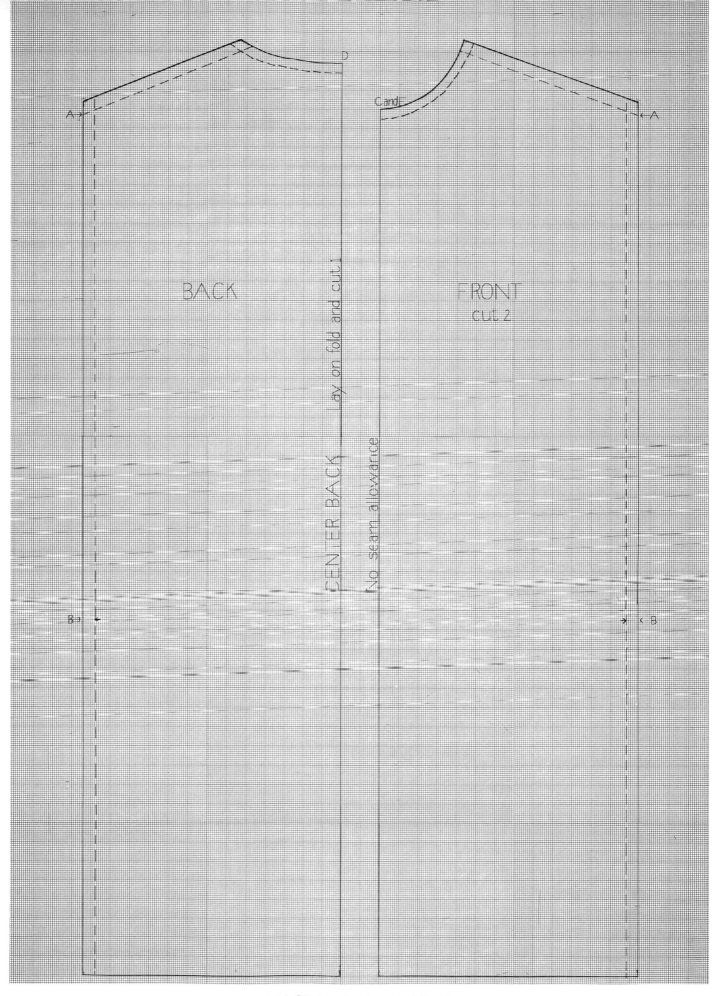

BACK

FRONT
cut 2

CENTER BACK · Lay on fold and cut 1

No seam allowance

A→

A←

B→

B←

C and D

D

MAGYAR COAT—LARGE

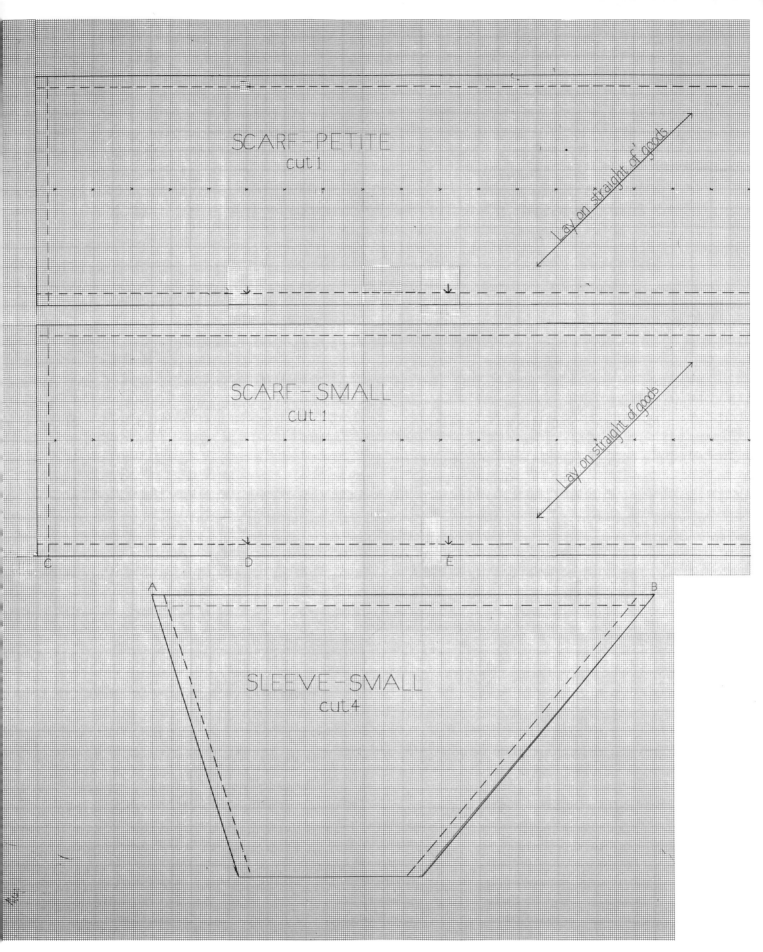

MAGYAR COAT—PETITE AND SMALL

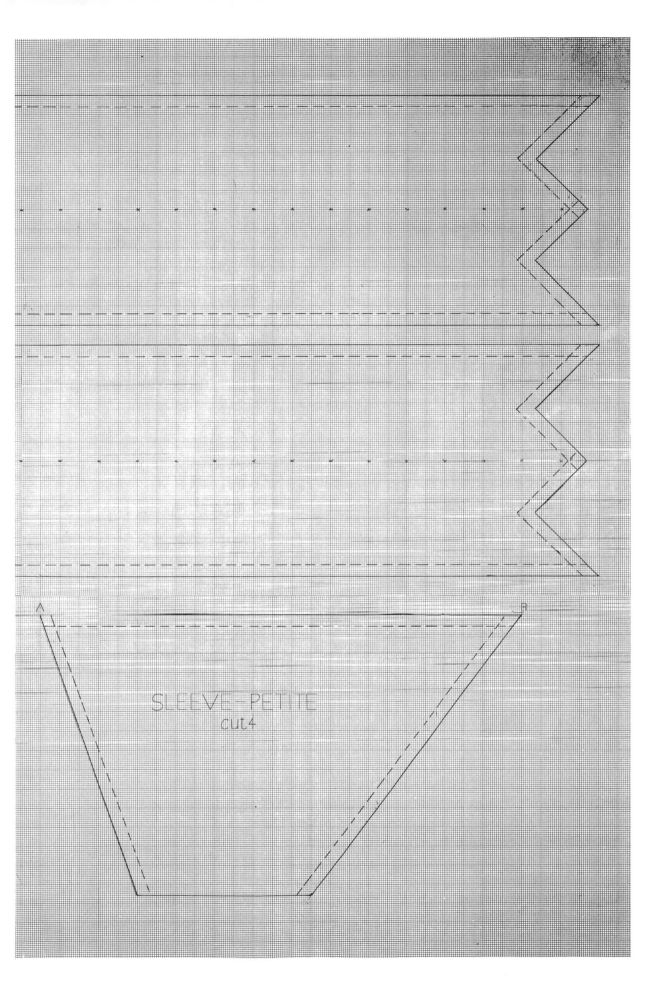

SLEEVE-PETITE
cut4

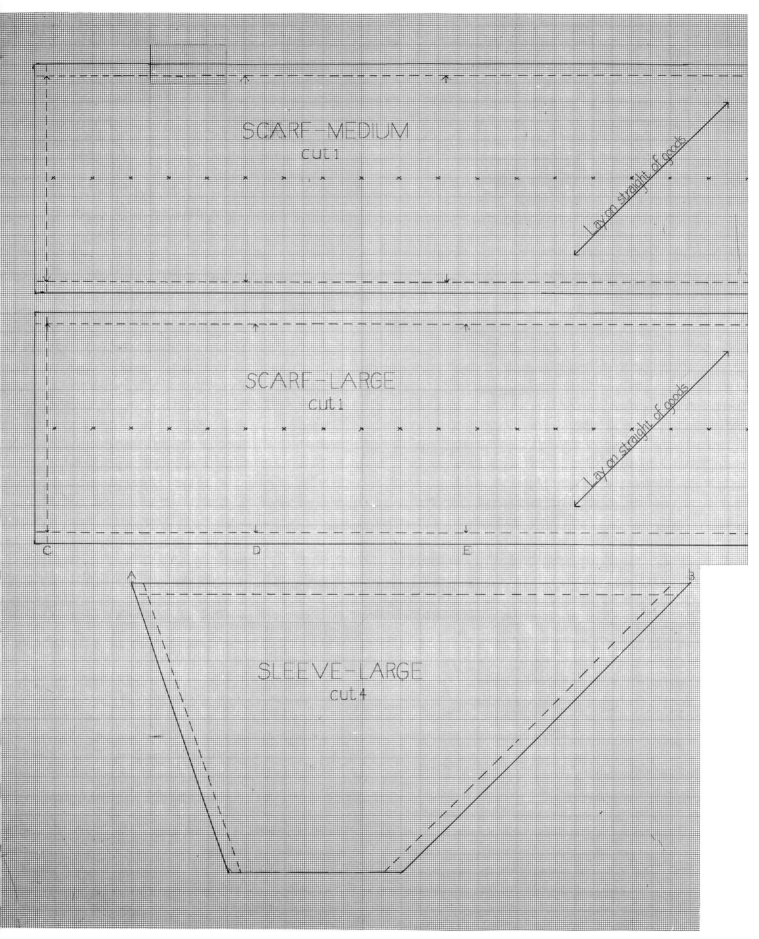

SCARE MEDIUM
cut 1

Lay on straight of goods

SCARE LARGE
cut 1

Lay on straight of goods

C   D   E

A   B

SLEEVE LARGE
cut 4

MAGYAR COAT—MEDIUM AND LARGE

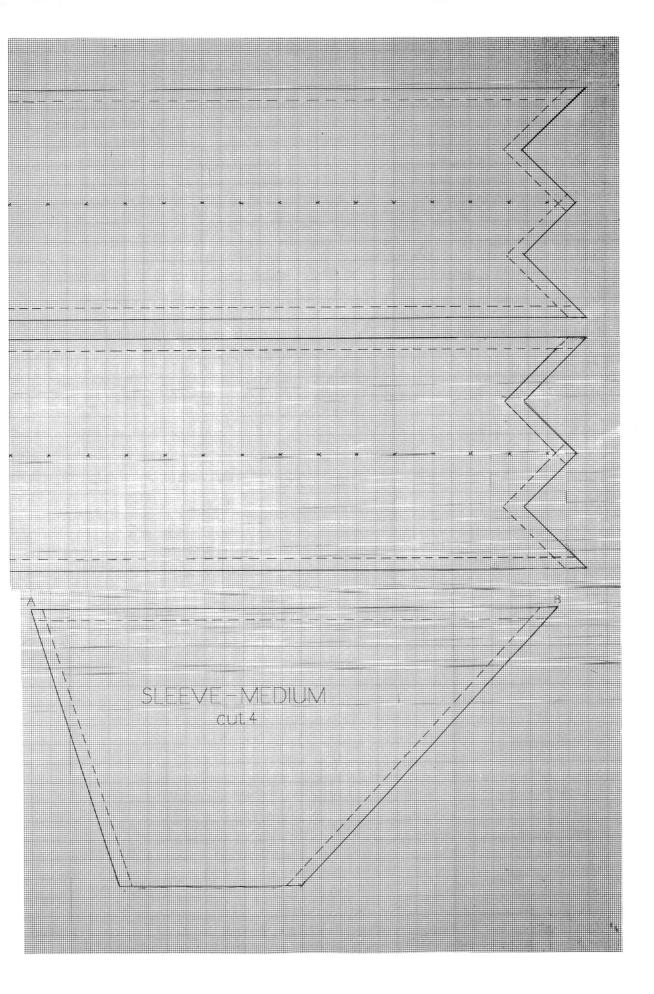

SLEEVE – MEDIUM
cut 4

BIAS SLIP DRESS

TWO PIECES
Front   cut two
Back   cut two

Lay both pattern pieces on your fabric. Lay them with the center front and the center back on the true bias, that is, at a 45-degree angle to the lengthwise grain of the fabric. To find this angle easily, use a right-angle triangle and a yardstick. Place one side of the triangle along the selvage of the fabric. Press one edge of the yardstick against the hypotenuse of the triangle. The ruler will then lie on the true bias, at a 45-degree angle to the selvage (see diagram page 14).

Cut two fronts and two backs. You may have to piece them (see diagram).

Cut about 10 yards of 1¾-inch-wide bias binding from the dress fabric, or from a contrasting fabric. See detailed instructions on bias binding, page 14.

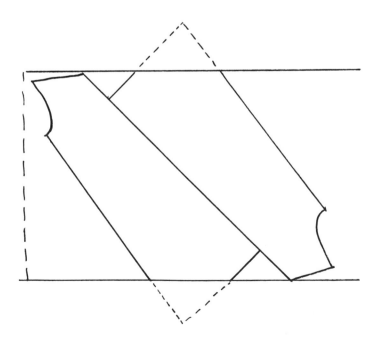

Center front and center back on true bias of fabric.

Sew the bias binding to the neck edges of the two back pieces. Press the binding away from the back pieces. Sew the center back seam, including in it the ⅜ inch at the neck edge where the binding has been sewn to the back pieces. Sew the two front pieces to the back along the side seams. Press the scams open. Sew bias binding all around the dress. Sew bias binding to the armholes. Press the binding away from the dress.

Sew the shoulder seams across the points, and include in the seam the ⅜ inch of binding on each side of the points.

Fold free edge of bias binding toward inside of dress to meet seamed edge of binding and edge of garment. Fold again, and pin folded edge of bias binding so that the folded edge meets the machine-stitched line joining the binding to the garment. Pin in place. Slip stitch folded edge of bias binding to the machine-stitched seam line.

With dress still inside out, lay the two center fronts together, one on top of the other bound edge. Pin in place. Use buttonhole stitch to join the two bound center front edges together.

Make a bias tube belt for the dress, using bias binding. Fold the bias strip lengthwise down its center. Sew a seam ¼ inch away from the raw edges. Turn the tube right side out using a turner made just for this purpose.

Use the bias slip dress pattern to make the tank top for a patchwork evening dress like the one shown in Plate 10. Use it for blouses to be worn over Indian pants. Use it for floor-length dresses. Simply shorten or lengthen the muslin pattern.

If you prefer dresses cut on the straight grain of the fabric, lay the center front and the center back of the pattern parallel to the selvage, which is the lengthwise edge of the fabric.

Note Sew four no. 4 lead weights to the bottom of the blouse when you make it on the bias. Sew the weights to the seams at center front, center back, and at the two sides, to make the blouse hang correctly. Attach lingerie guards to the shoulder seams to keep the blouse's shoulder straps in place.

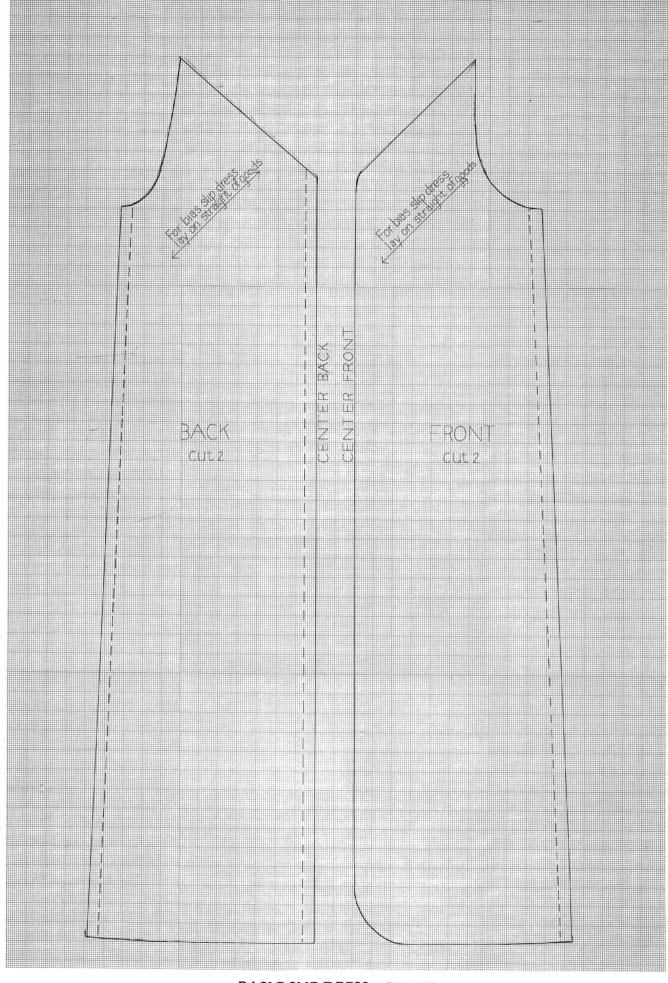

For bias slip dress
lay on straight of goods

For bias slip dress
lay on straight of goods

BACK
cut 2

CENTER BACK

CENTER FRONT

FRONT
cut 2

BASIC SLIP DRESS—PETITE

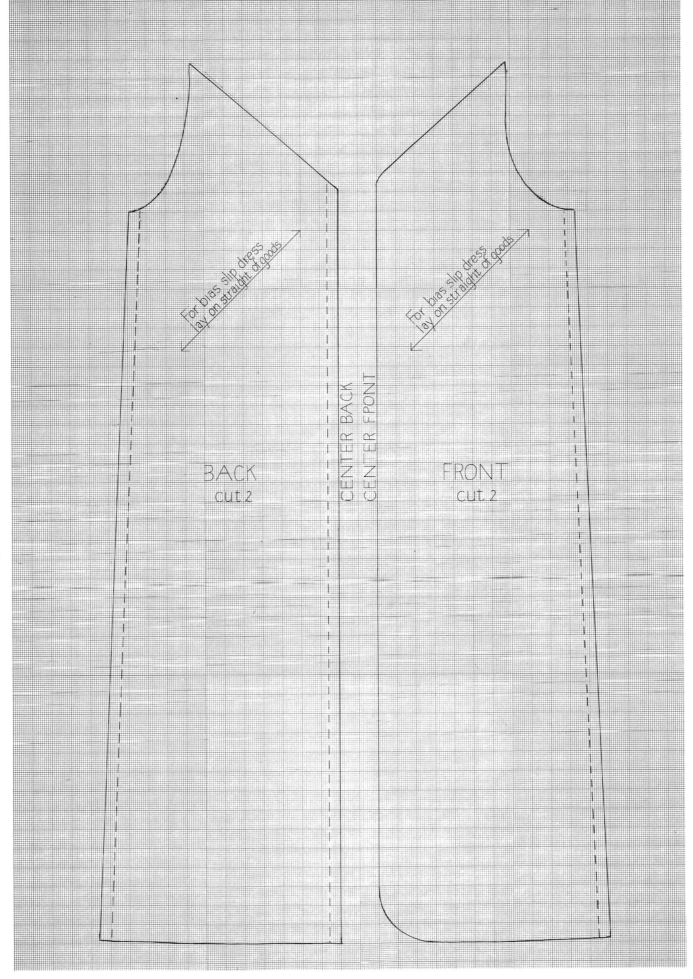

For bias slip dress
lay on straight of goods

For bias slip dress
lay on straight of goods

CENTER BACK

CENTER FRONT

BACK
cut 2

FRONT
cut 2

BASIC SLIP DRESS—SMALL

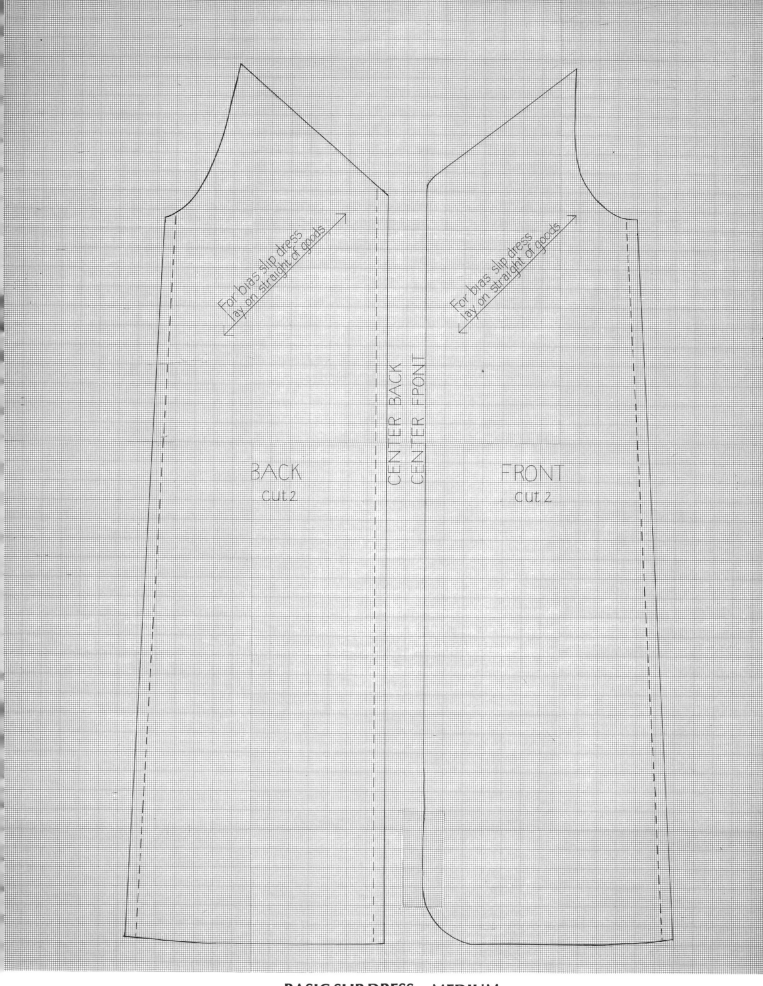

For bias slip dress
lay on straight of goods

For bias slip dress
lay on straight of goods

CENTER BACK
CENTER FRONT

BACK
cut 2

FRONT
cut 2

BASIC SLIP DRESS—MEDIUM

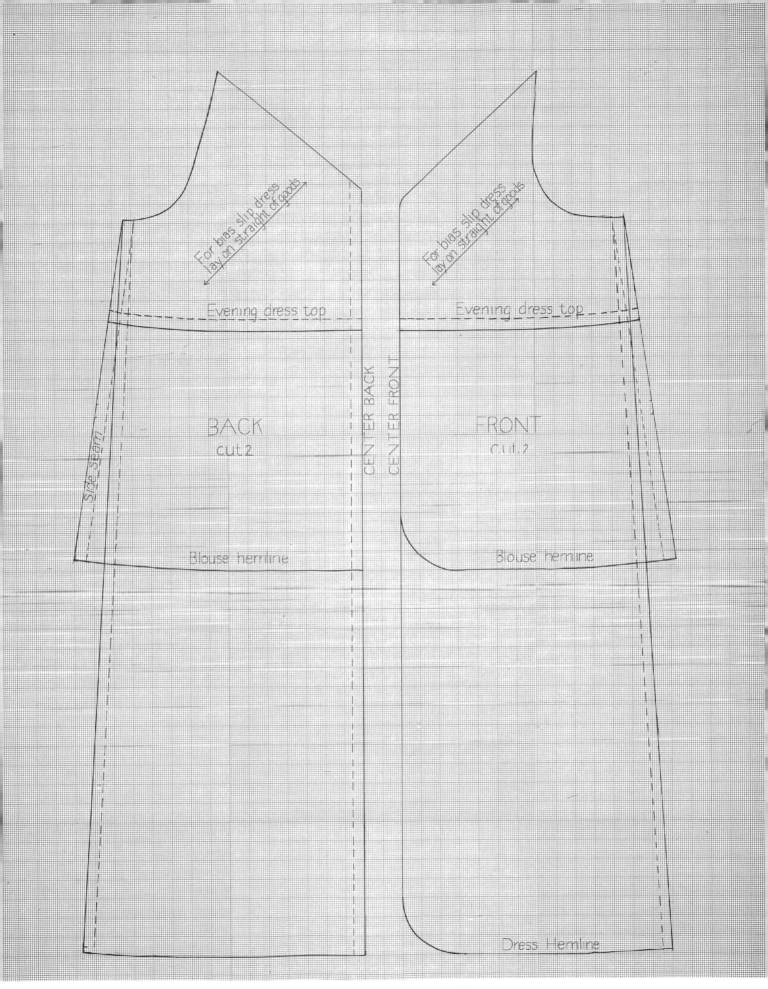

BASIC SLIP DRESS—LARGE

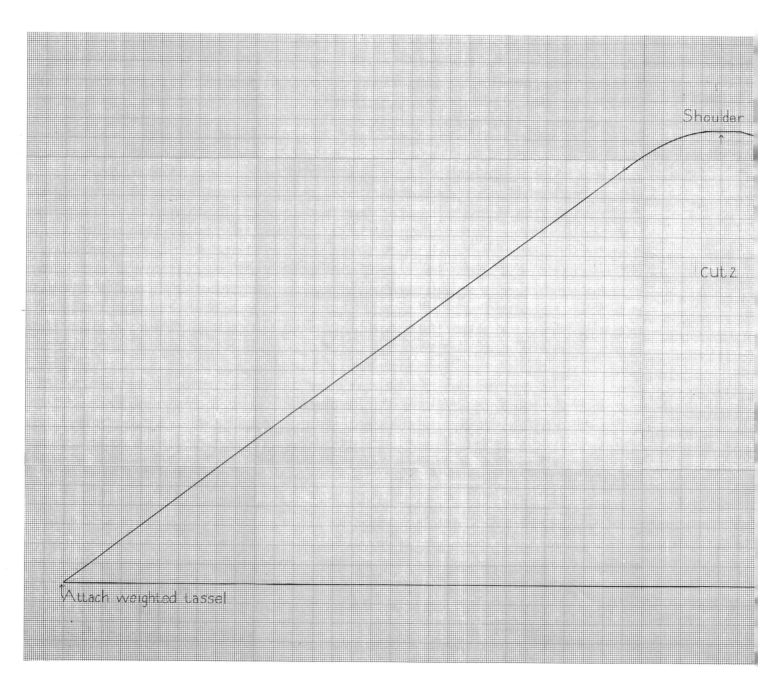

Shoulder

cut 2

Attach weighted tassel

TRIANGULAR SLEEVE FOR EVENING DRESS

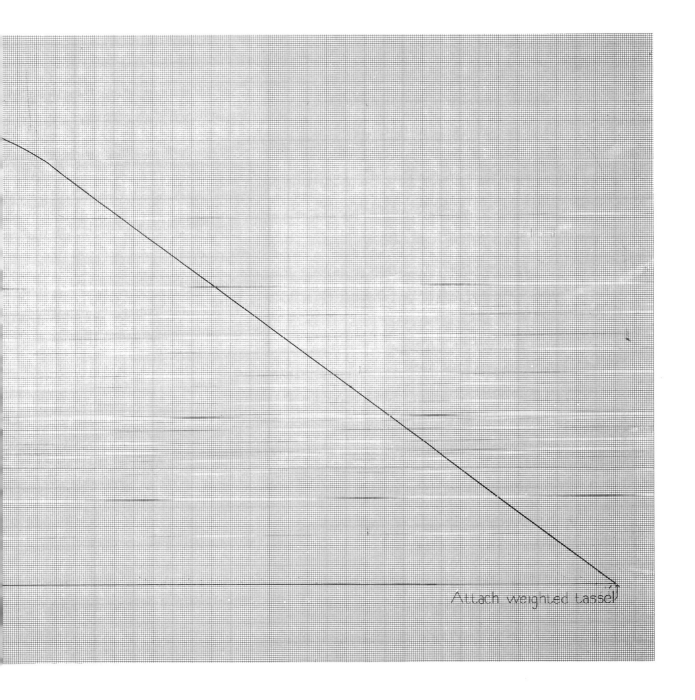

Attach weighted tassel

47

FOUR-GORE SKIRT

ONE PIECE
Back and front   cut four

Cut two back and two front gores, using the same pattern piece for all four gores of the skirt.

Sew center front and center back seams. Sew side seams. (Add pockets in side seams if you like.) Press all seams open.

Finish waist and bottom edges of skirt with bias binding.

Sew bias binding to inside of skirt where the two rows of dotted lines on the pattern indicate. This casing is for an elastic waistband, or a bias tube belt which can come out and tie at the skirt's center front seam.

Fore-gore skirt.

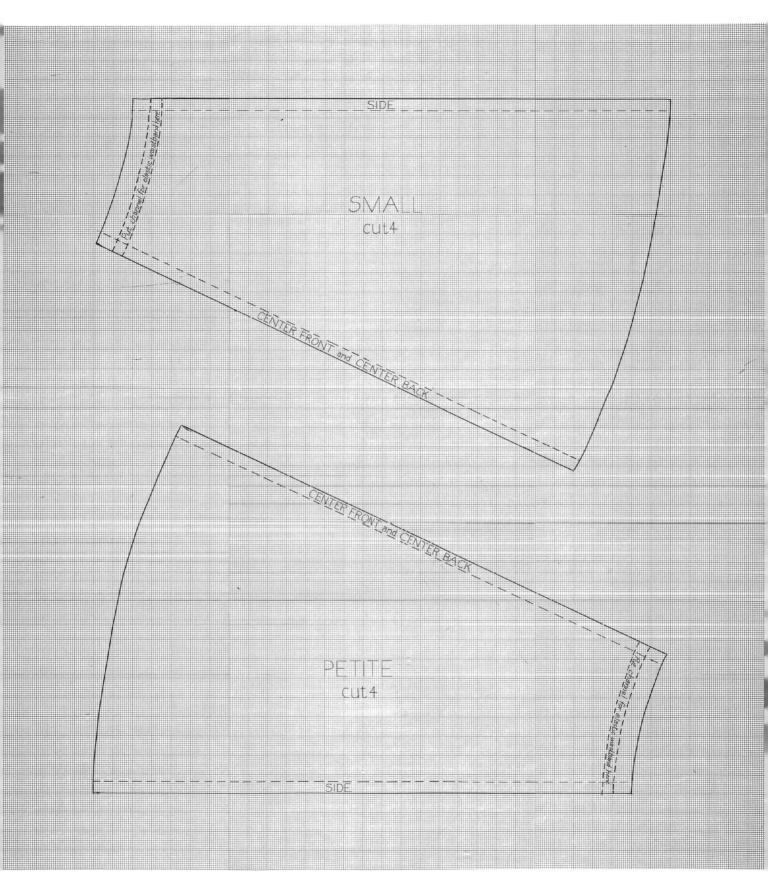

SIDE

Cut channel for elastic waistband here

SMALL
cut 4

CENTER FRONT and CENTER BACK

CENTER FRONT and CENTER BACK

Cut channel for elastic waistband here

PETITE
cut 4

SIDE

FOUR-GORE SKIRT—PETITE AND SMALL

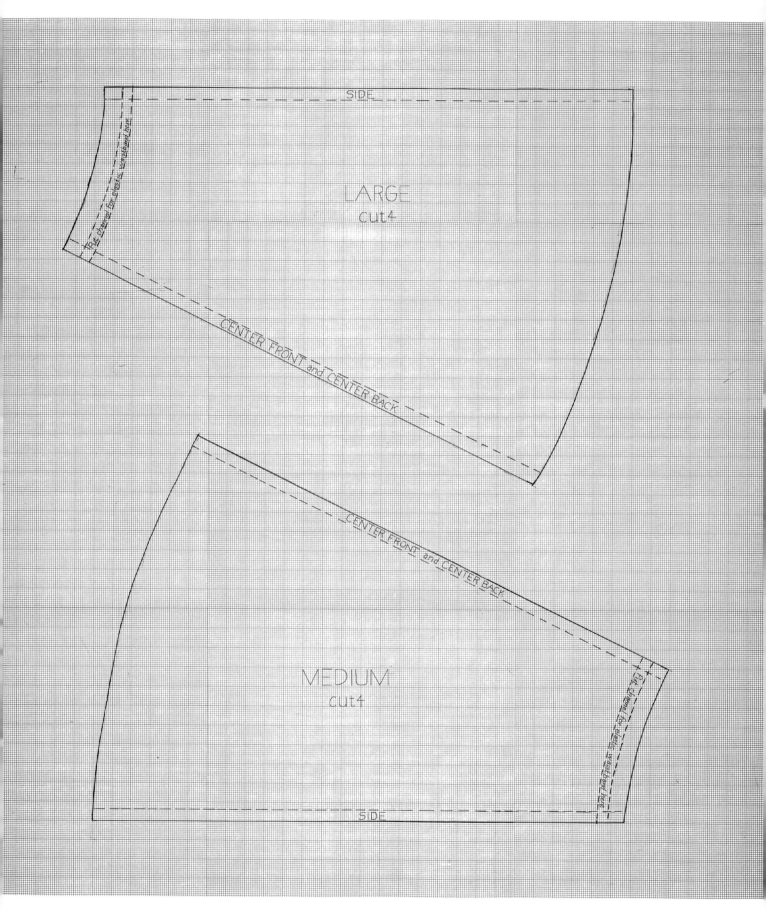

FOUR-GORE SKIRT—MEDIUM AND LARGE

CAPE

TWO PIECES
Front cut two
Back cut two

Front   Lay center front of pattern along selvage, or on lengthwise grain of fabric. Cut right and left front pieces. Use very wide fabric, or piece it.

Back   Lay center back of pattern along selvage, or lengthwise grain of fabric. Cut right and left back pieces. If necessary, piece each part of the back at lower side seam corner.

Sew center back seam. Press seam open. Sew side seams, and press open. Finish raw edges of cape with bias binding. Use fur hooks and eyes to join center front.

If you want to add a scarf collar, use the pattern given with the Magyar coat pattern. In this case, use the outline given for the neckline of the Magyar coat to cut the neckline of the cape.

See Plate 22.

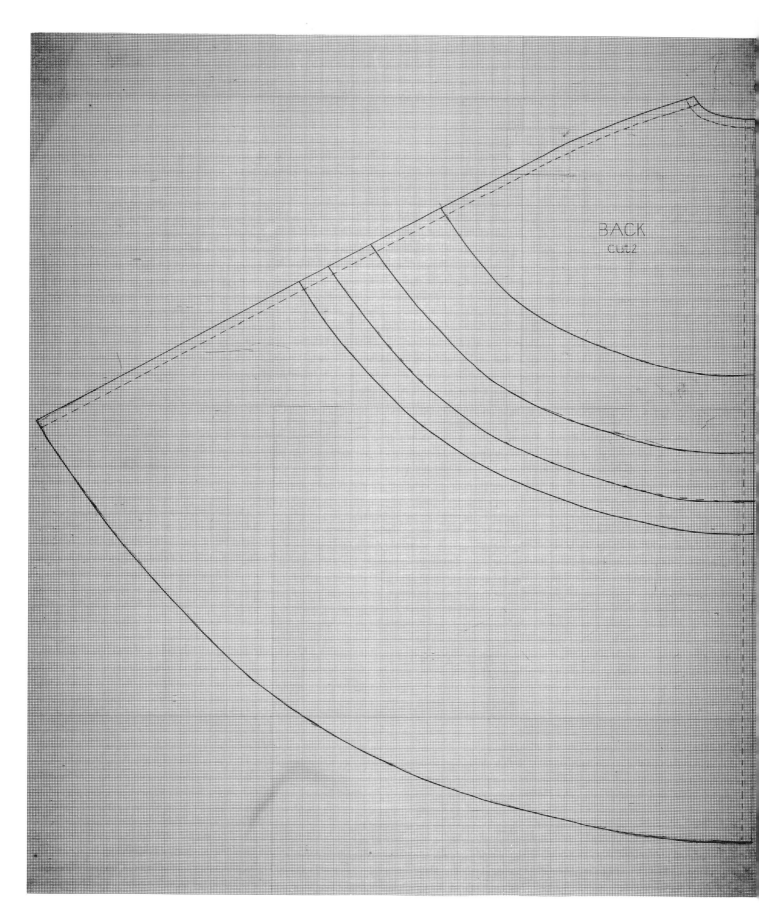

BACK
Cut 2

STREET-LENGTH CAPE—ONE SIZE FITS ALL

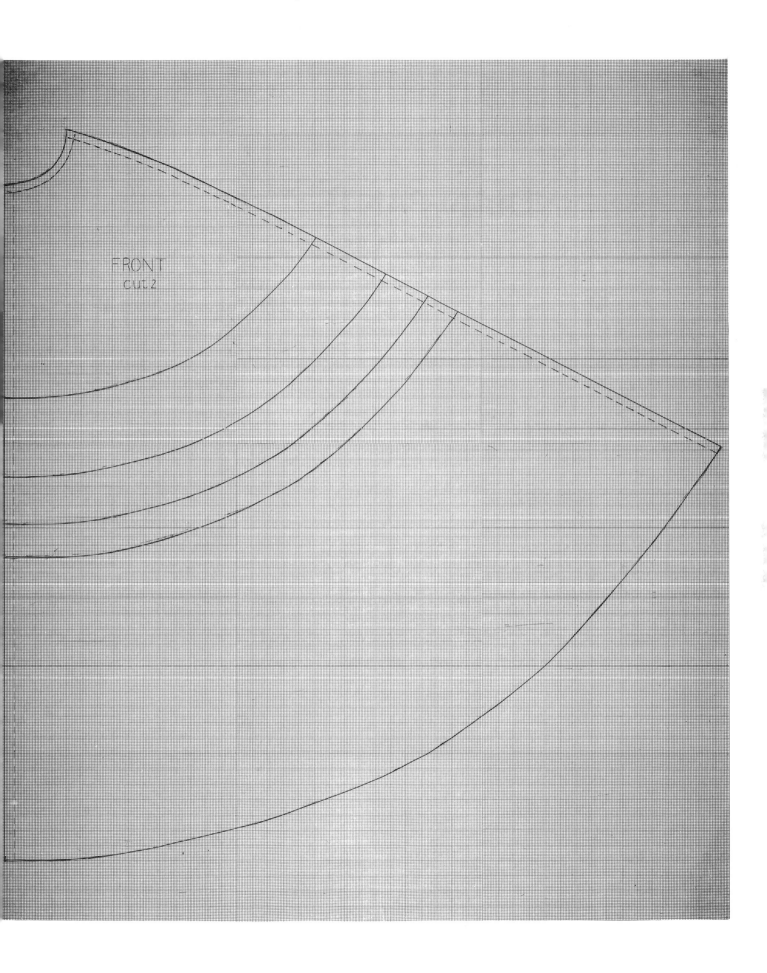

FRONT
CUT 2

INDIAN PANTS

ONE PIECE
Front and back   cut one

Sew bias binding to the sides of the panel, from *A* to *A*. These will be the leg openings. Press the bias binding away from the panel. Fold the panel on its crosswise fold line, from *D* to *D*. Sew side seams from *B* to *C*, that is, from leg openings to waist. Turn in and finish bias binding at leg openings.

Sew 2½-inch bias binding all around waistline. Press binding away from pants. Turn bias strip toward inside of pants to make a casing for an elastic band, ⅜ inch wide, cut to your waist measurement. Sew bias binding to machine-stitched line. Run elastic through the casing. Lap an inch at one end of the elastic band over an inch at the other end of the elastic. Sew by hand or with a zigzag stitch on the machine.

Indian pants

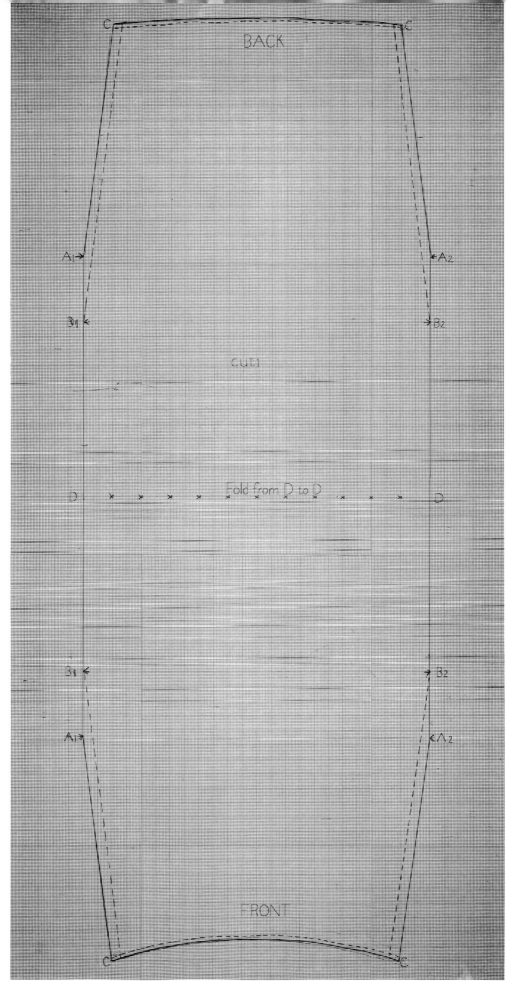

INDIAN PANTS—PETITE

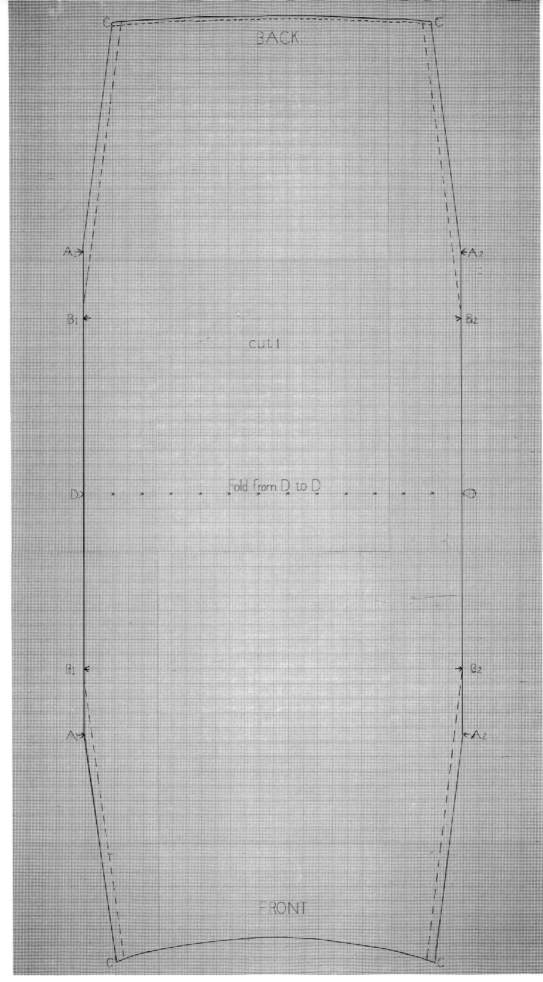

BACK

C   C

A₁→   ←A₂

B₁←   →B₂

cut 1

D→ · × · × · × Fold from D to D × · × · × ←D

B₁←   →B₂

A→   ←A₂

FRONT

C   C

INDIAN PANTS—SMALL

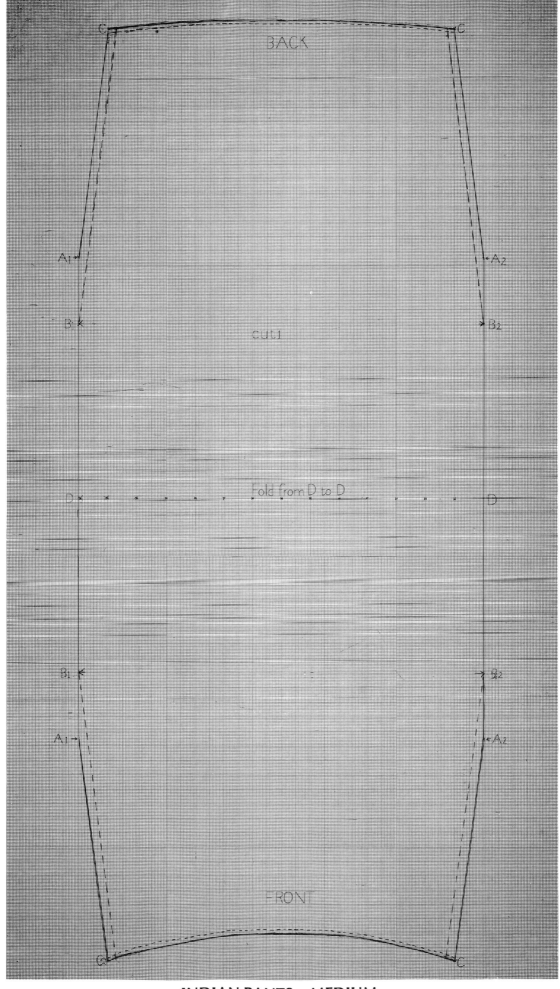

INDIAN PANTS—MEDIUM

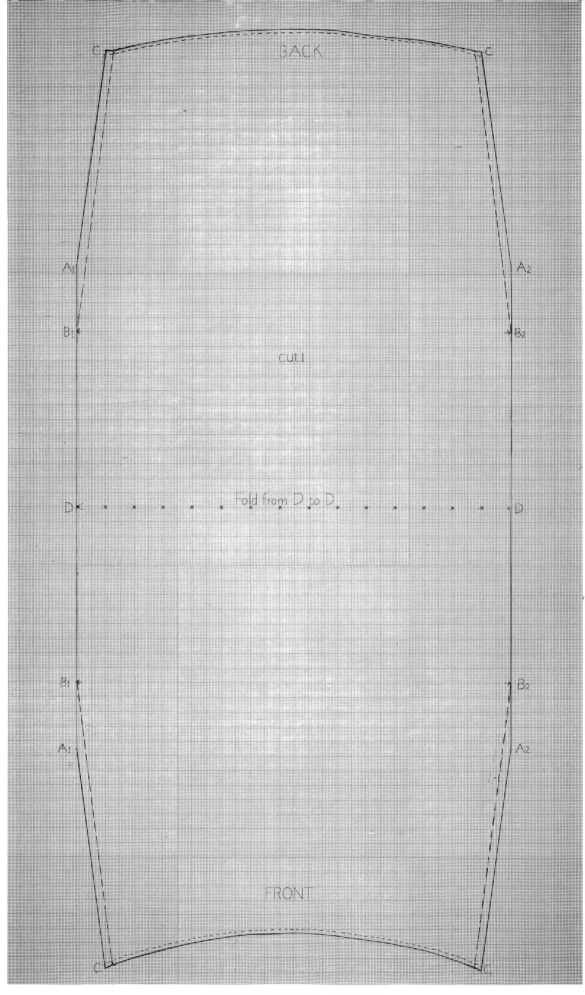

INDIAN PANTS—LARGE

TABARD

TWO PIECES
Front   cut one
Back   cut one

Front   Lay center front of pattern along lengthwise fold of fabric and cut one piece.

Back   Lay center back of pattern along lengthwise fold of fabric and cut one piece.

Interline and line each piece, then quilt.

Sew right front shoulder to right back shoulder. Press seam open. Trim seam allowance to ⅜ inch. Cover seam with a strip of bias binding. Turn edges of bias strip under and slip stitch these folded edges to the lining.

Finish the raw edges of the tabard with bias binding. Use buttons, snaps, hooks and eyes, or Velcro on left shoulder to join back to front.

Attach bias spaghetti ties to sides of front and back panels at waist level or slightly above it. The tie at the right side will remain tied. The tie at the left side will be tied when the tabard is being worn.

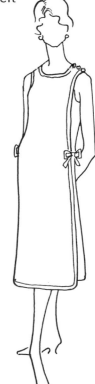

Tabard

59

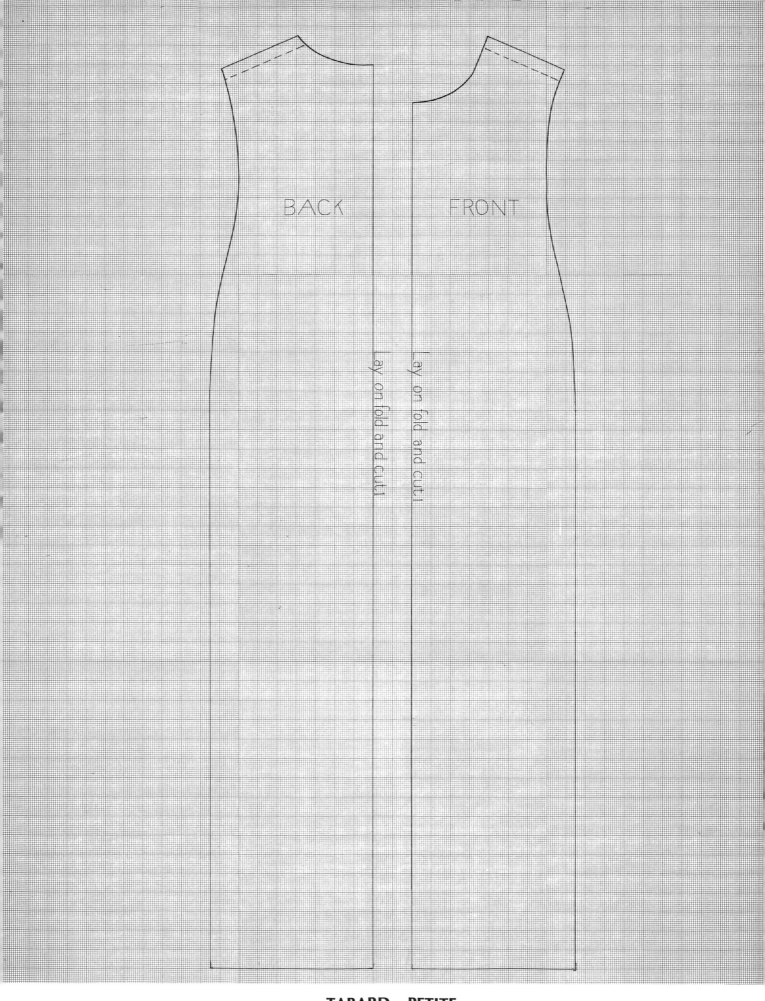

BACK

FRONT

Lay on fold and cut1

Lay on fold and cut1

TABARD—PETITE

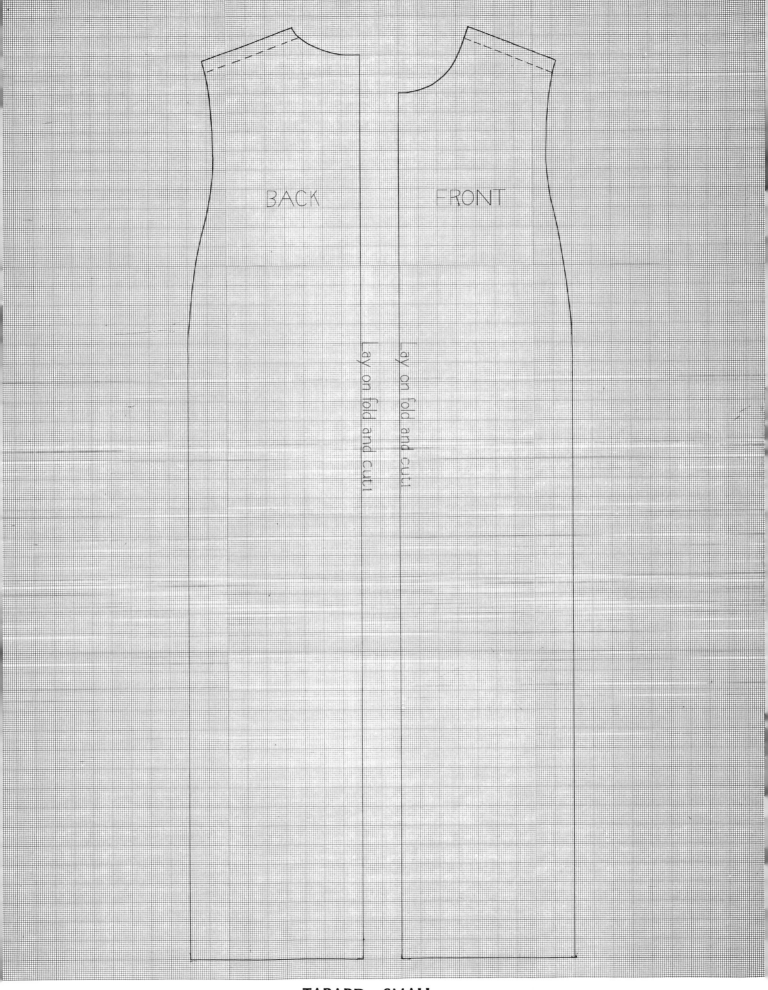

BACK

FRONT

Lay on fold and cut1

Lay on fold and cut1

TABARD—SMALL

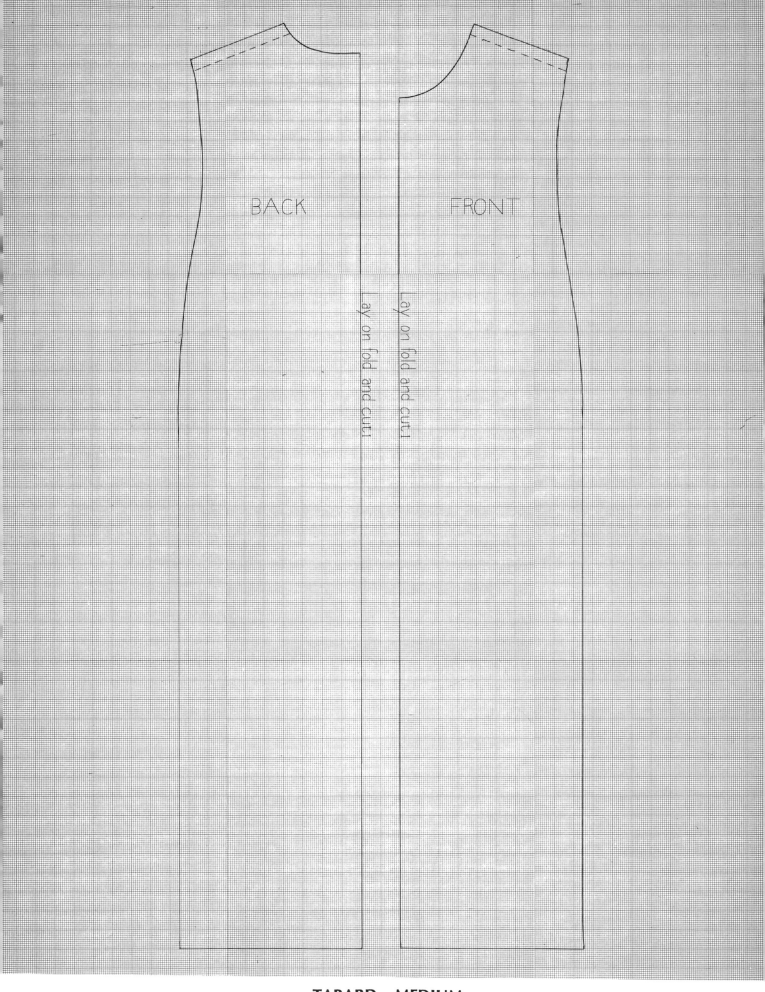

BACK

FRONT

Lay on fold and cut 1

Lay on fold and cut 1

TABARD—MEDIUM

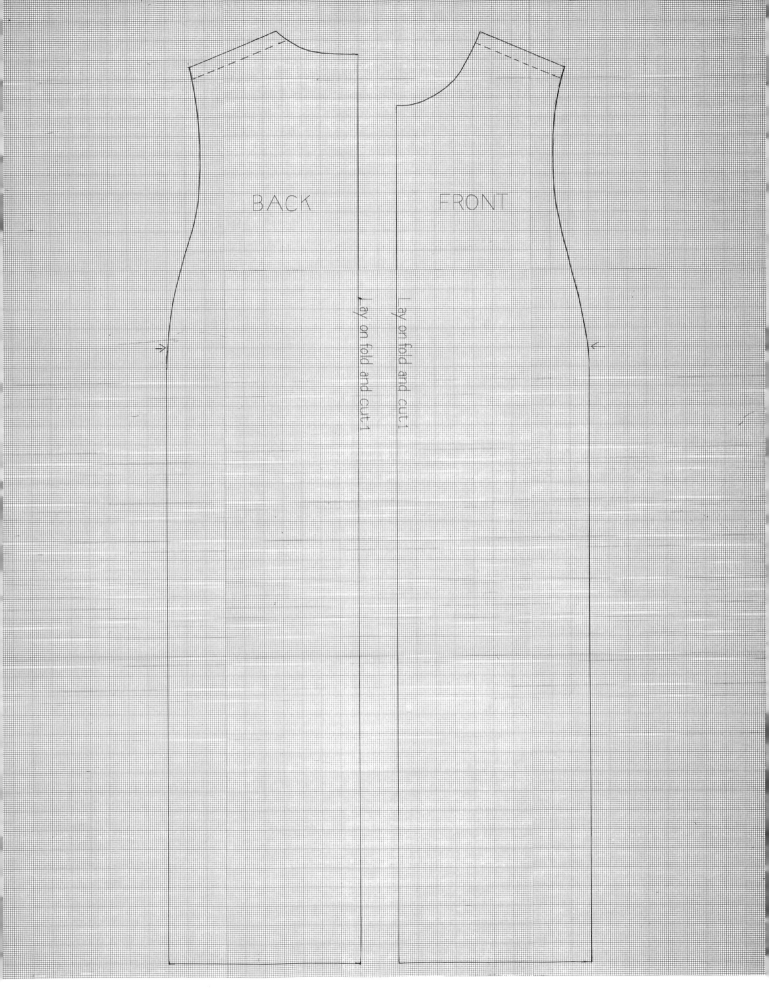

BACK FRONT

Lay on fold and cut 1

Lay on fold and cut 1

TABARD—LARGE

KITE

ONE PIECE
Front and back cut two

Cut two pieces of fabric following the outline of each pattern piece. Sew shoulder seams.

Sew the center back seam from neckline to bottom of kite. Sew side seams. Finish kite with bias binding.

The pattern may be cut with a 2-inch separation at the shoulder line, as shown in Plate 11, where appliquéd circles hold the fronts to the back at shoulder and wrist. In this case, cut off 2 inches at the shoulder line of the pattern and finish these shoulder-to-wrist edges with bias binding.

The kite may be sewn down the center front—to knee level—with button-hole stitch. See instructions for the bias slip dress (page 40). Or you may want to tie the center fronts together, slightly below the bustline—at empire waist level—with long, thin spaghetti ties made of bias binding, or close the front with a single decorative frog button.

The kite can be worn over floor-length slip dresses, or regular or ankle-length Indian pants topped by a bias blouse, loosely tied with a spaghetti tube belt.

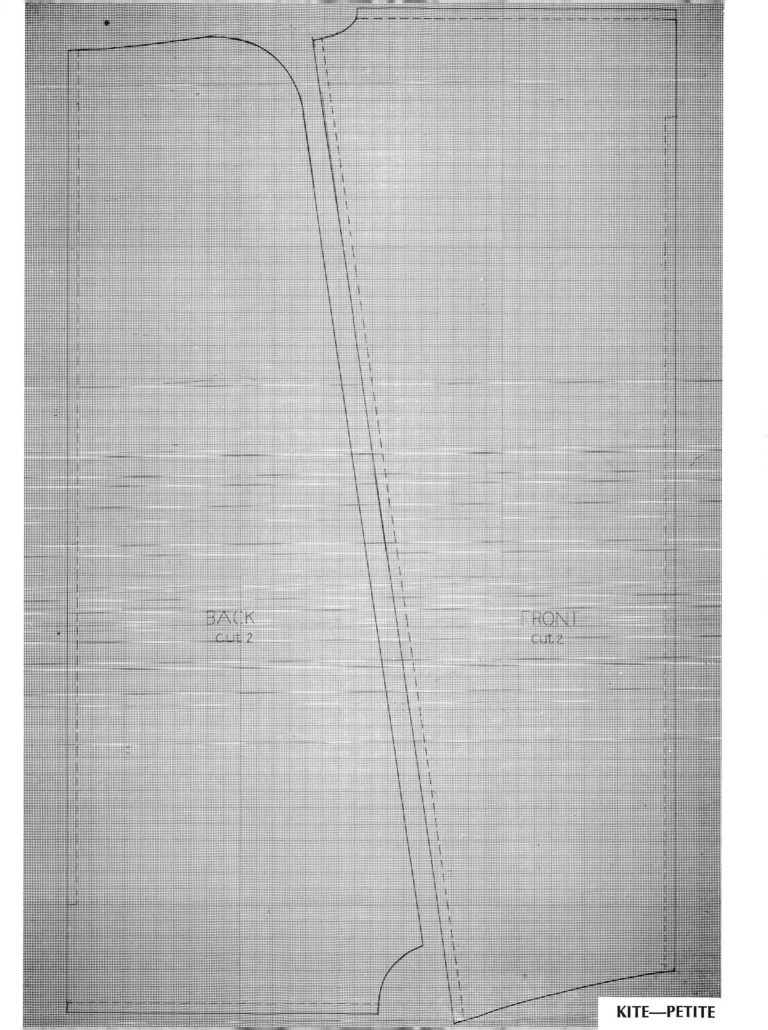

BACK
Cut 2

FRONT
cut 2

KITE—PETITE

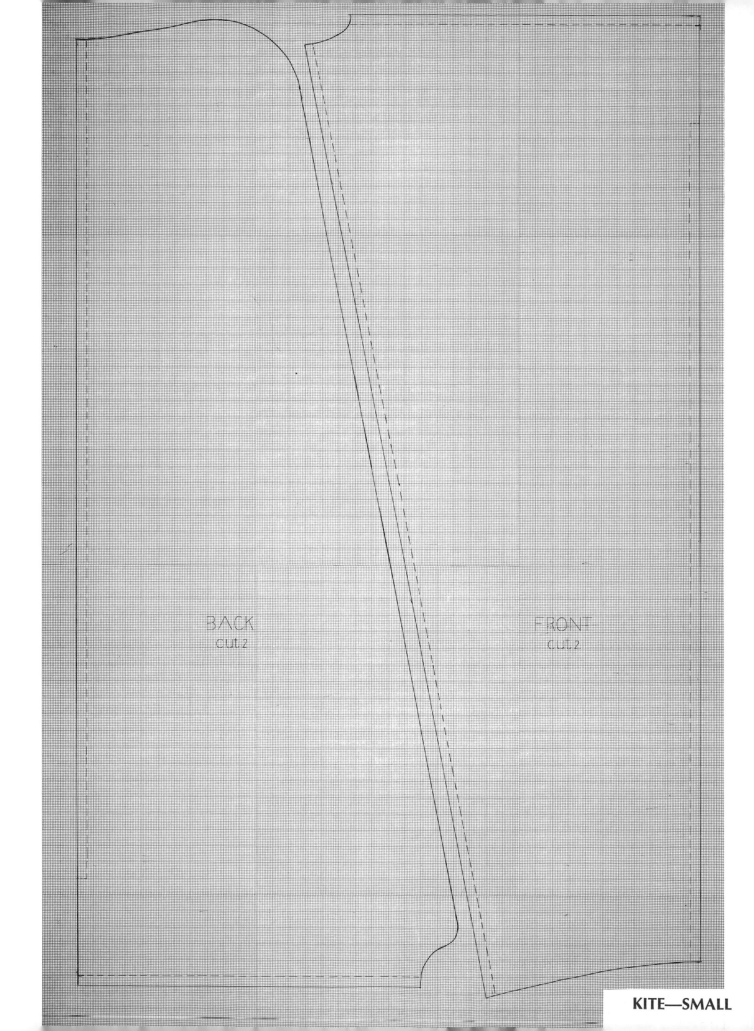

BACK
cut 2

FRONT
cut 2

KITE—SMALL

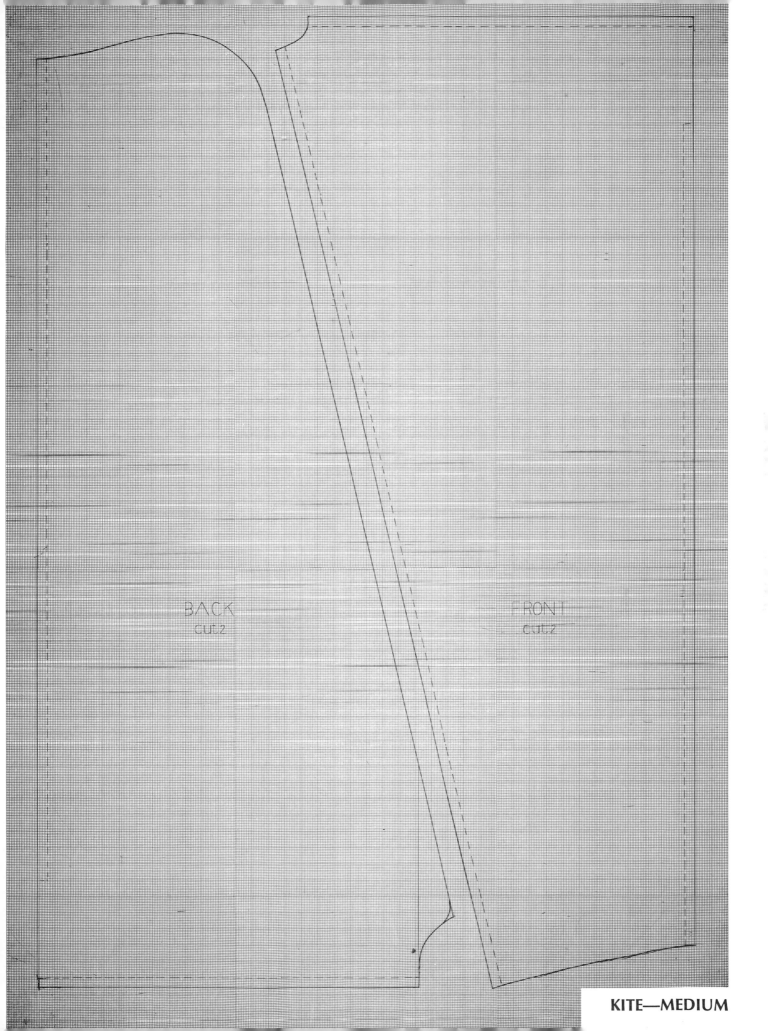

BACK
cut 2

FRONT
cut 2

KITE—MEDIUM

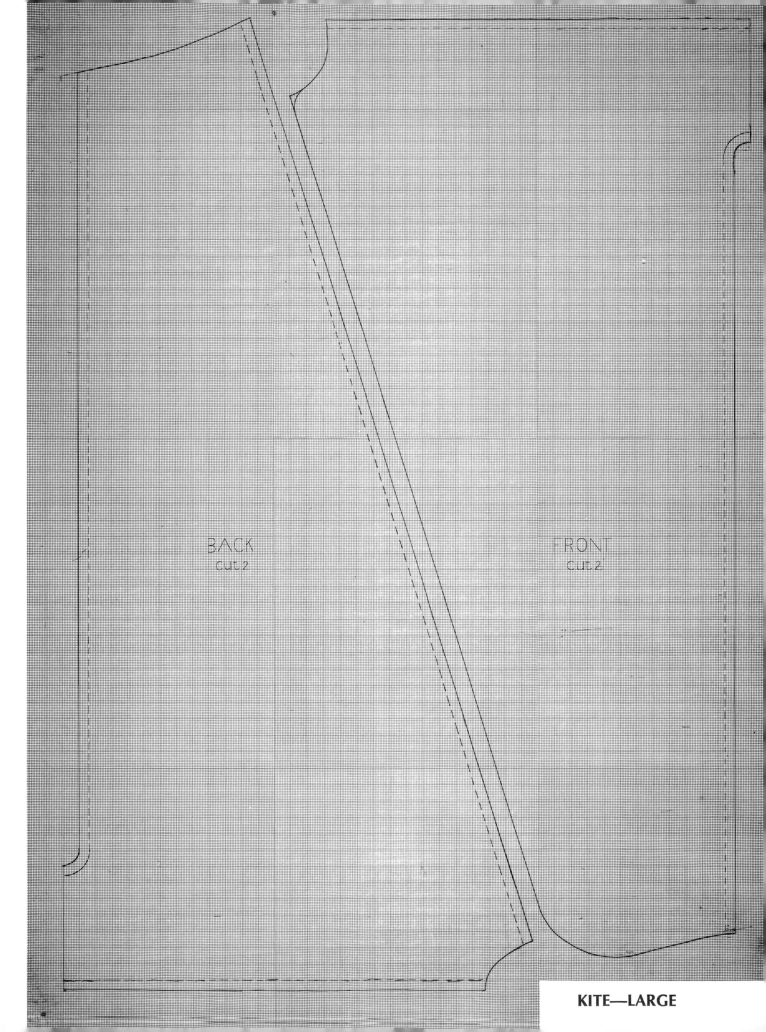

BACK
cut 2

FRONT
cut 2

KITE—LARGE

KARATE JACKET

THREE PIECES
Front   cut two
Back   cut one
Sleeve   cut two

Front   Lay center front of pattern along lengthwise grain of fabric and cut left and right front pieces.

Back   Lay center back of pattern along lengthwise fold of fabric and cut one piece, or add ⅝-inch seam allowance to pattern, at center back, and cut two pieces, left and right back.

Sleeve   Lay center of sleeve pattern along lengthwise grain of fabric and cut left sleeve and right sleeve.

Sew shoulder and side seams. Press seams open. Sew sleeve seams. Press seams open. Sew sleeves to jacket. Clip seams at underarms, and press seams toward sleeves, or trim armhole seams to ⅜ inch and bind with bias binding. Finish raw edges of jacket and sleeves with bias binding. Make spaghetti tubing for tying jacket fronts.

Jacket left front crosses over jacket right front. Sew a short tie to jacket left and right front at A on jacket pattern. Sew a short tie on inside of jacket left front. Sew ties on jacket left front at B on jacket pattern. Sew ties on outside of jacket right front at C and D to hold jacket together. Make a flat tie belt to go loosely around waist. Make belt holders on right and left sides of jacket.

See Plate 14.

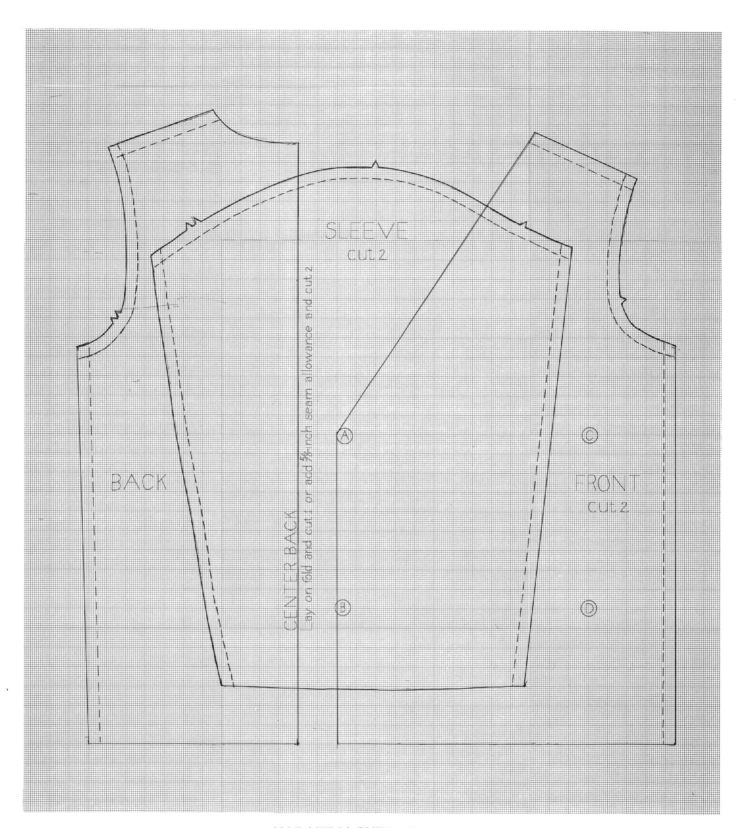

SLEEVE
cut 2

BACK

CENTER BACK
Lay on fold and cut 1 or add ⅝-inch seam allowance and cut 2

Ⓐ

Ⓑ

FRONT
cut 2

Ⓒ

Ⓓ

KARATE JACKET—SMALL

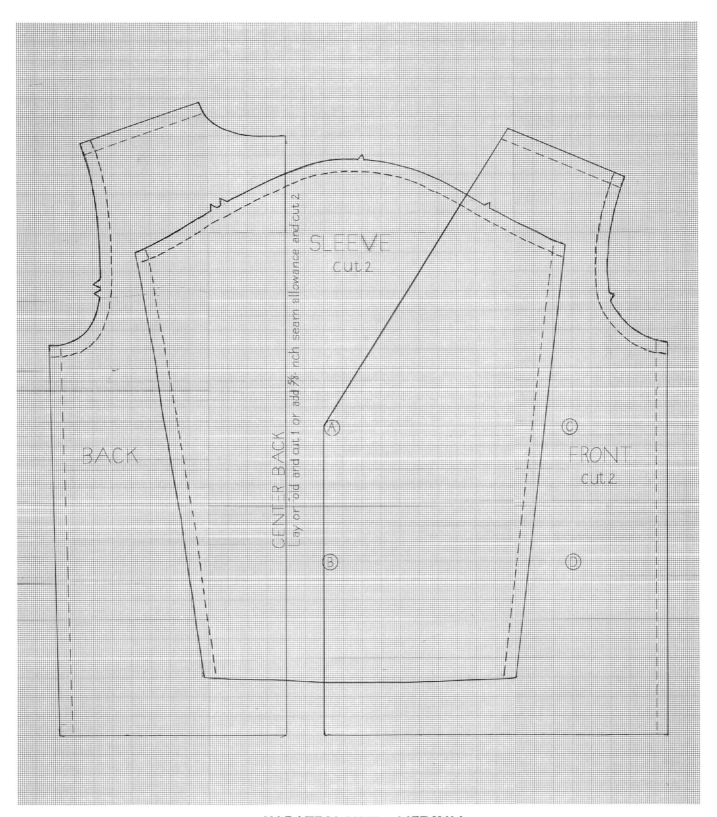

BACK

SLEEVE
cut 2

FRONT
cut 2

CENTER BACK   Lay on fold and cut 1 or add 5⁄8 inch seam allowance and cut 2

Ⓐ

Ⓑ

Ⓒ

Ⓓ

KARATE JACKET—MEDIUM

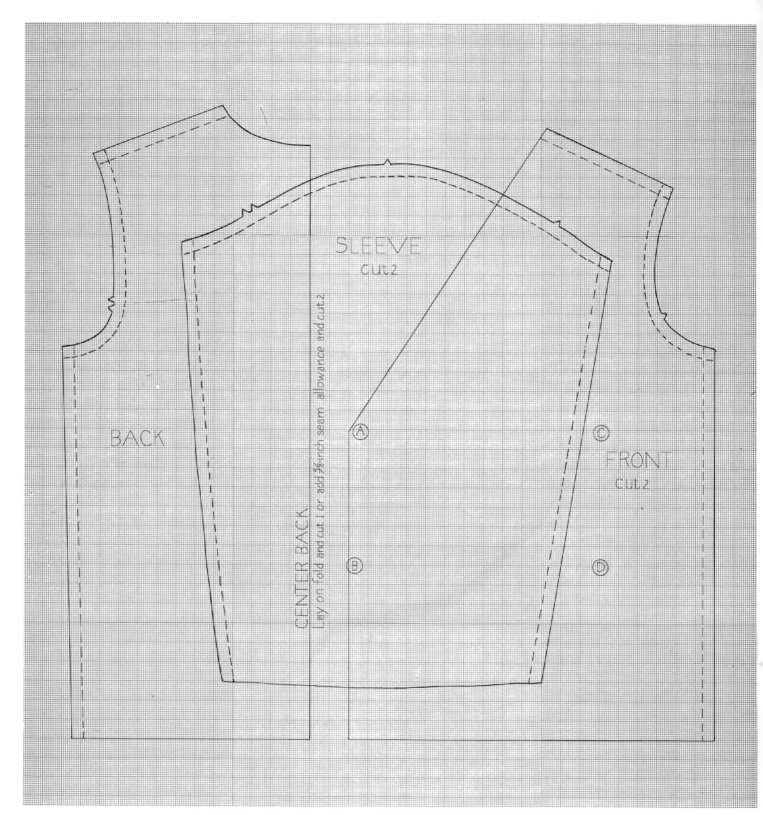

KARATE JACKET—LARGE

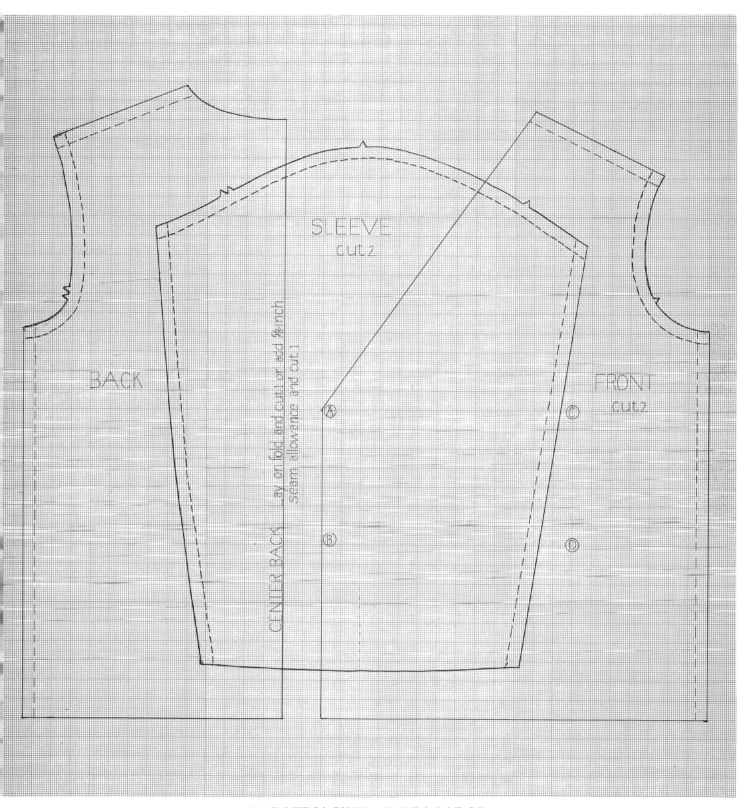

BACK

SLEEVE
cut 2

FRONT
cut 2

CENTER BACK   lay on fold and cut 1 or add ⅝-inch seam allowance and cut 1

Ⓐ

Ⓑ

Ⓒ

Ⓓ

KARATE JACKET—EXTRA LARGE

DOFUKO

Cut or patch four strips twice as long as the length of the strips shown in the pattern outlines. Cut or patch one strip half as long as the four long ones. This strip will be for the center back, from neckline to floor. Cut or patch four shorter strips for the sleeves. Cut or patch one strip for the collar. Mount each strip of patchwork on underlining and hand stitch the patchwork to the mounting along every seam, joining patches together.

Put the strips together as shown in the diagram. The collar is not shown; it is applied later.

Sew together the strips making up the body of the robe. Sew together the strips making up the sleeves. Sew the sleeves to the robe only at the shoulders, lengthwise from A to A. Fold the robe across the shoulders, and with the inside out, stitch the side seams, from D to E. Stitch the lower part of the hanging sleeves, from the wrist, B, down around the curve and across the bottom of the sleeve to C.

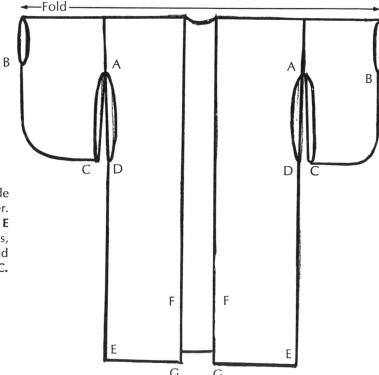

Stitching guide for dofuko, inside out. Sew sleeves to shoulder. Sew side seams from **D** to **E** and on **A** to **A,** hanging sleeves, from wrist opening at **B,** around curve and across bottom to **C.**

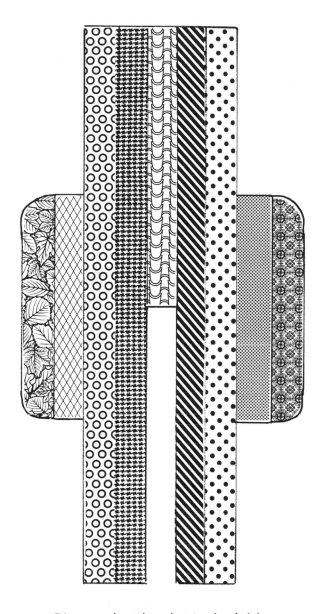

Diagram of patchwork strips for dofuko.

Cut a lining to fit the robe. Sew it together following the same stitching guide as the one given for the robe.

With the right sides of the robe and the lining facing each other, and with their wrong sides out, sew the lining to the robe from F to G, then all around the hemline, from G to G, and then up the other side to F. Clip the seam allowance at F. Turn the robe and lining both right sides out through the F-to-F opening. Baste the lining to the robe from F to F with the seam allowance exposed. Sew one edge of the collar to the seam allowance on the robe. Sew from F to F. Fold under the ⅝-inch seam allowance at the raw edge of the collar. Turn the collar toward the lining of the robe and slip stitch the folded edge of the collar to the lining from F to F. Turn in the seam allowance at the open ends of the folded collar and close them with slip stitch.

Turn in the seam allowances on the lining and the robe at underarm openings and at wrist openings, and slip stitch them together, lining to robe, on the sleeve from A to C to A, and from B to B, and on the robe from A to D to A. See Plate 1.

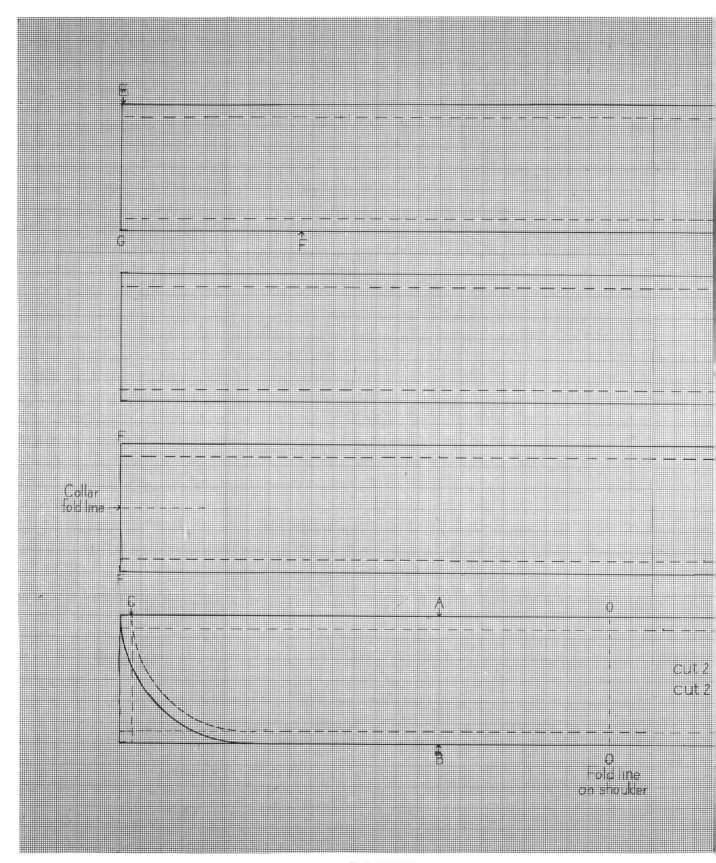

DOFUKO

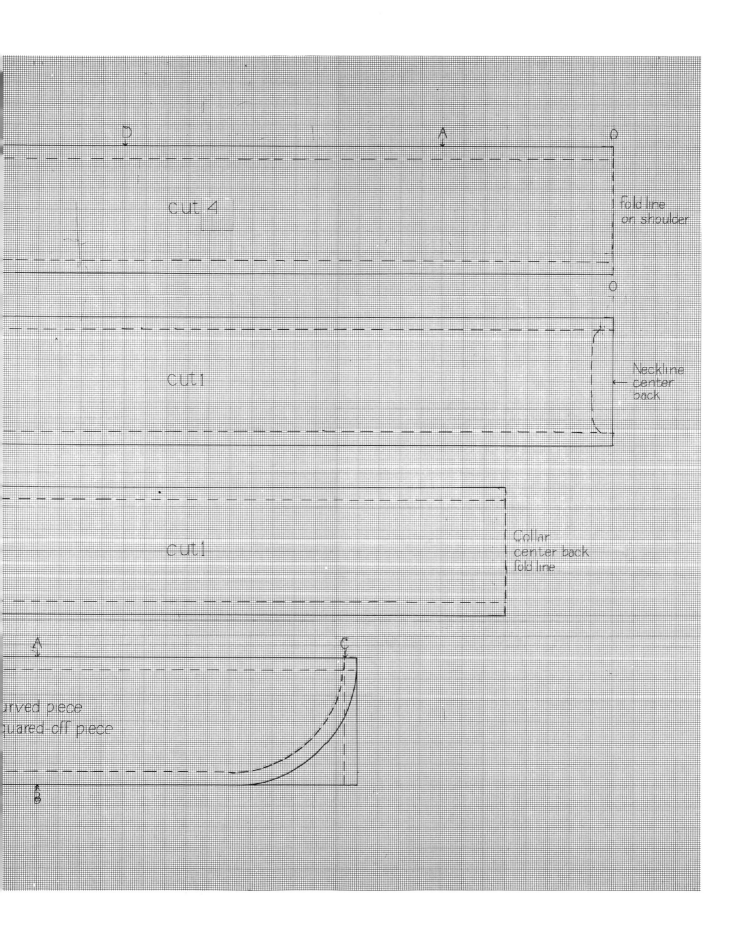

cut 4

fold line
on shoulder

cut1

Neckline
center
back

cut1

Collar
center back
fold line

urved piece
quared off piece

MAN'S CAFTAN

FIVE PIECES

Back	cut two
Front	cut two
Side panel	cut four
Sleeve	cut two
Pocket	cut four

Sew a side panel to the front and back of each sleeve, from *A* to *B*. Sew center back seam. Sew center front seam. Sew pockets to sides of fronts between *C* and *D*. Sew pockets to side front panels facing toward fronts between *C* and *D*. Sew fronts to backs at shoulders. Sew sleeves, with their front and back side panels, to front and back. Then sew seam around each pocket, *C* to *D*. Sew underarm seam on sleeve from wrist to underarm curve, then down the sides of the caftan, joining the front and back side panels.

Finish raw edges of the caftan with bias binding. If you want a neck front opening and a slit at the center front from knee to bottom of caftan, or at the sides, from knee level to the bottom of the caftan, cut off the seam allowance for the slits, and finish with bias binding.

See Plate 20.

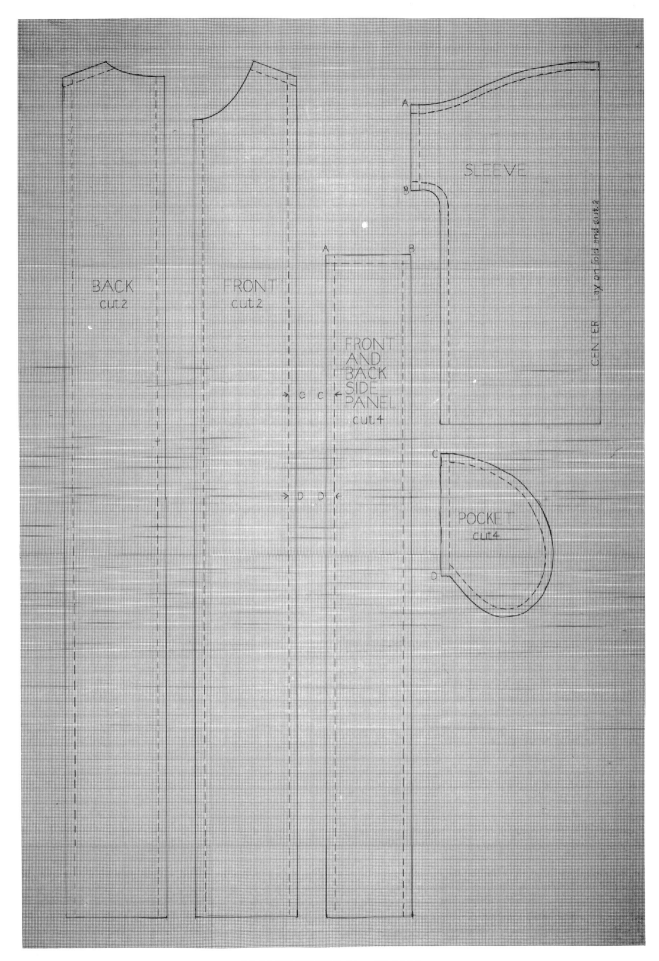

MAN'S CAFTAN—SMALL

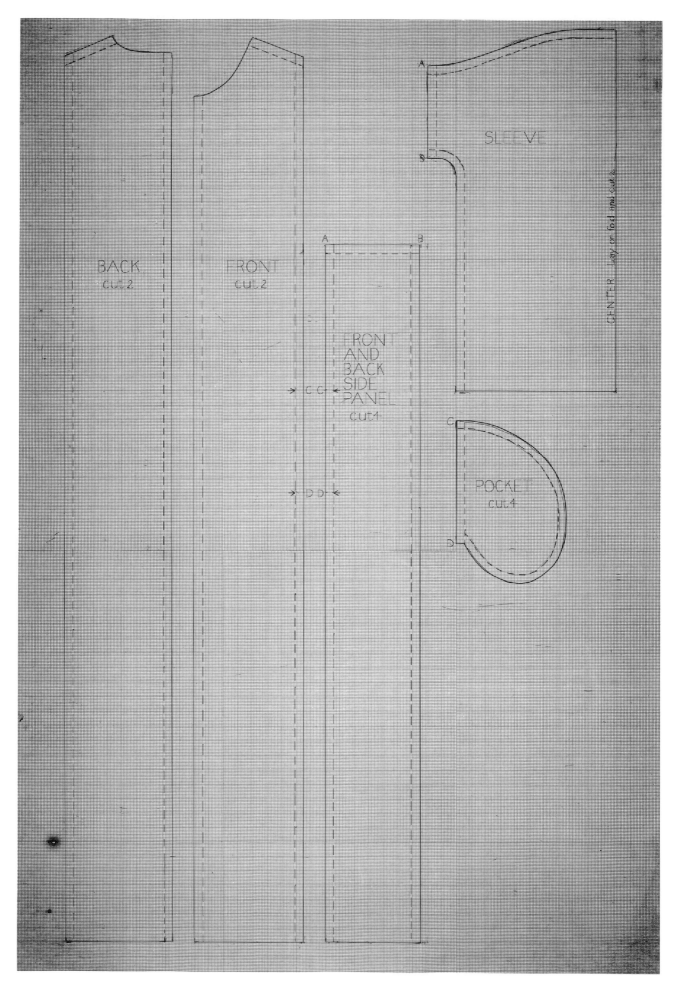

MAN'S CAFTAN—MEDIUM

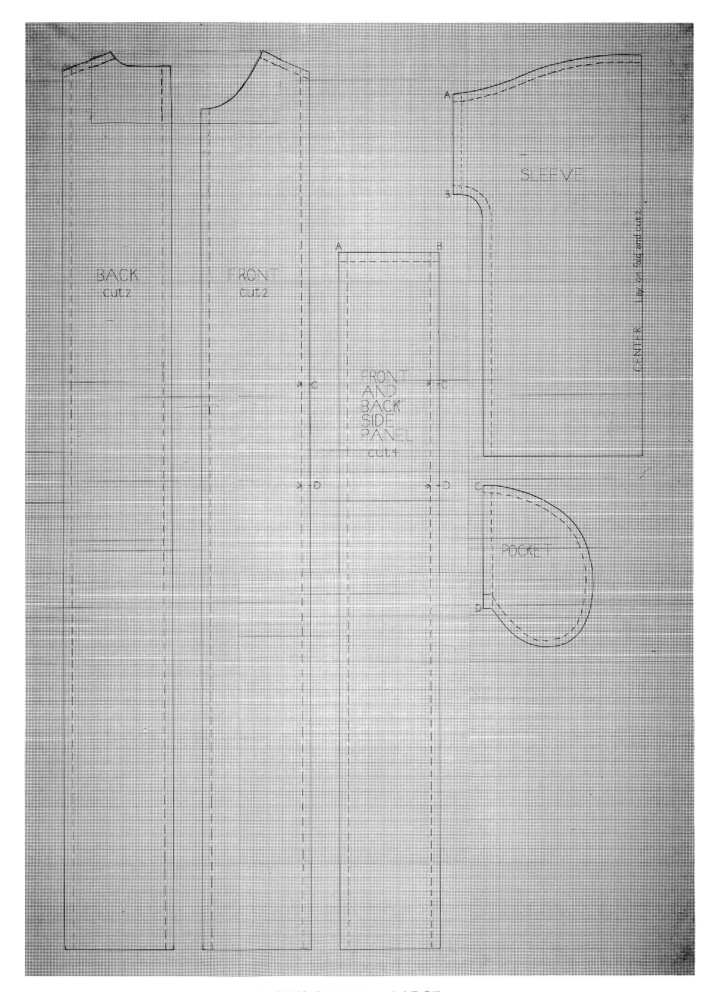

MAN'S CAFTAN—LARGE

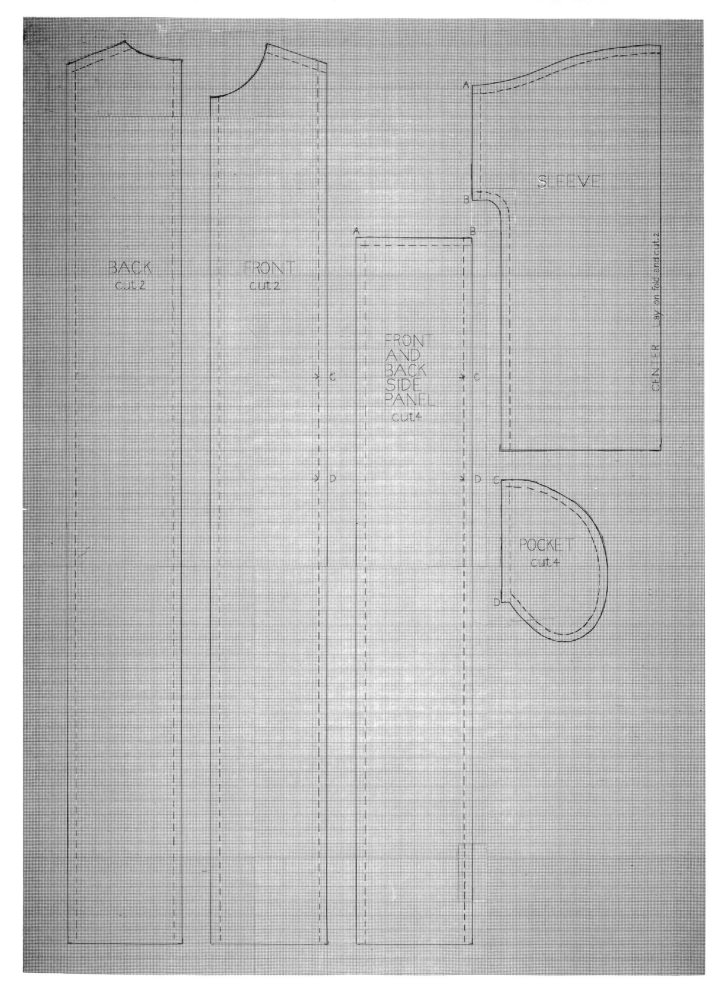

MAN'S CAFTAN—EXTRA LARGE

KANGAROO SHIRT

FIVE PIECES
For men or women

Back   Lay on center seam of patchwork and cut one side, then the other, or lay on fold of fabric and cut one.

Front   Lay on center seam of patchwork and cut one side, then the other, or add ⅝-inch seam allowance at center front of pattern and cut two.

Pockets   Cut two.

Sleeves   Cut two.

Collar   Cut two of lining fabric.

Open center front seam at neckline, from D to A. Clip seam allowance at A.

Open patchwork seams on front from B to C for pockets. Clip seam allowances at B and C. Attach pockets. If you want one pocket to go through from side to side, slip stitch the pocket front piece to the center front part of the shirt, from B to C on each side. Sew the pocket back to the side fronts of the shirt, from B to C. Sew the pocket back to the pocket front, from B to B and from C to C. If you want to make two separate pockets, use only half of the pocket pattern and add a ⅝-inch seam allowance on the center front of the pocket pattern, and cut four pieces.

Sew front of shirt to back of shirt at shoulder seams. Sew sleeves to shirt, from underarm across shoulder to underarm. Sew seam along under side of sleeve, around the underarm curve, and down the sides of the shirt.

Make a lining for the shirt using the same pattern pieces used for the shirt, but adding no pockets. With right side of lining facing right side of shirt, sew lining to shirt on both sides of neck opening, from D to A.

Baste lining to shirt around neckline. Sew collar lining to neckline. Sew collar to collar lining, right sides together. Turn collar right side out and slip stitch collar to shirt lining at neckline. Turn under seam allowances at sleeve hem and slip stitch lining to sleeve.

Make stitching line close to bottom of shirt for belt casing. Make bias tube belt. Run belt through casing. (Opening of casing is at center front, in the patchwork seam.)

Wear the shirt with a turtleneck sweater, with trousers or skirt.

Note: If you make the shirt from regular fabric, not patchwork, you may add ⅝ inch seam allowance to front and back and cut two pieces for each.

See Plate 15.

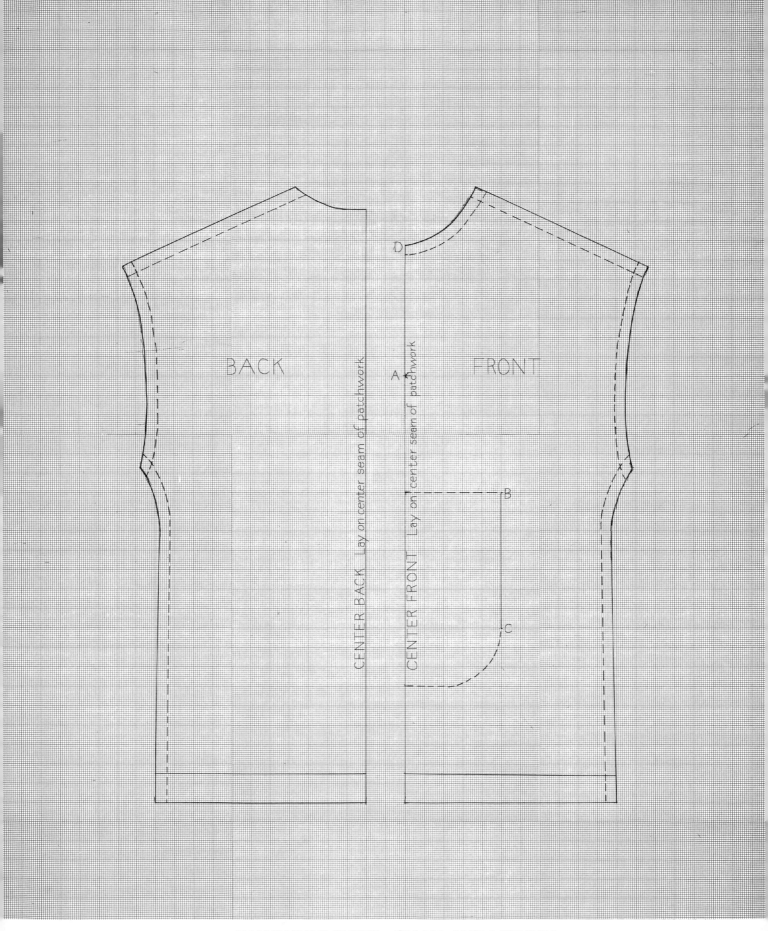

BACK

FRONT

CENTER BACK   Lay on center seam of patchwork

CENTER FRONT   Lay on center seam of patchwork

A

B

C

D

KANGAROO SHIRT—SMALL AND MEDIUM

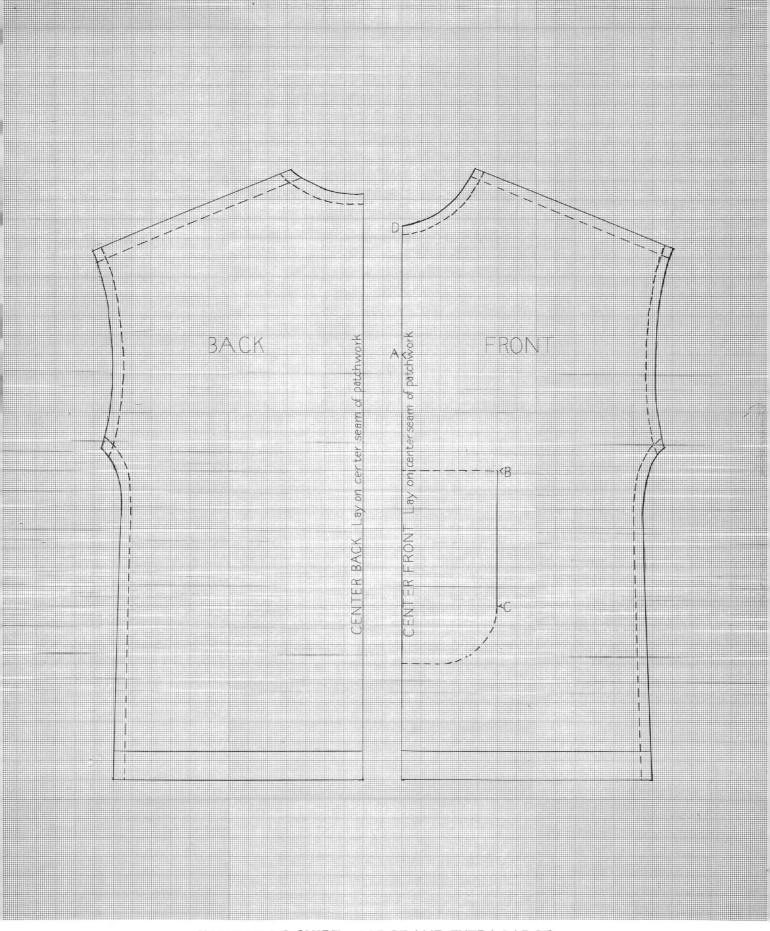

BACK

FRONT

CENTER BACK   Lay on center seam of patchwork

CENTER FRONT   Lay on center seam of patchwork

A

D

B

C

KANGAROO SHIRT—LARGE AND EXTRA LARGE

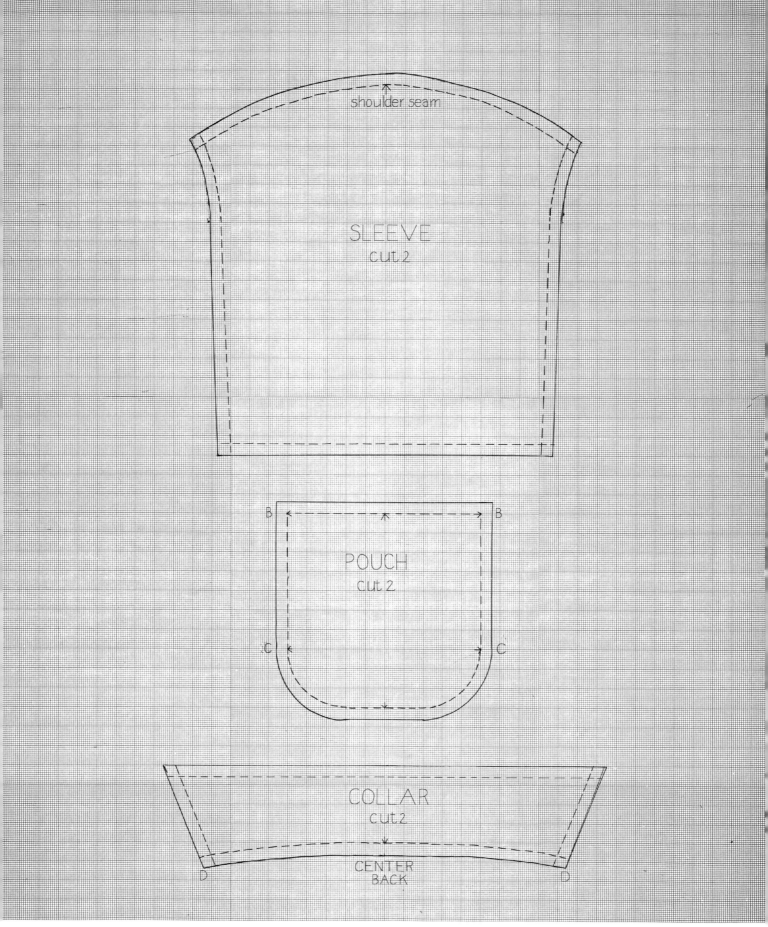

KANGAROO SHIRT—ALL SIZES

Patchwork Patterns

Each of the patchwork garments in this book was made with fabrics I gathered together with a specific color combination in mind. For most of the costumes I used about eighteen different fabrics, patterned, striped, and plain, in a tonal range from light to dark. I bought ½ yard of each type, except the lightest and darkest tones of which I bought a yard each, for they appear more often in the patching.

Beginning here, and continuing on the following pages, you will find detailed instructions for the five kinds of patchwork used in making the clothes illustrating this book.

JAPANESE SIXTEENTH-CENTURY PATCHWORK

This kind of patchwork is made of fabric cut into squares, rectangles, triangles, parallelograms, and trapezoids. These are sewn together to make long strips. The strips are then seamed together, side by side, and the resulting fabric is used with the strips running vertically. The effect created by the juxtaposition of the strips of patches reminds one of an abstract painting, or of an aerial view of rows of neatly tilled farmland fields.

There are few rules to follow when making this type of patchwork. I tried, however, to avoid placing two horizontal seams—on adjacent strips—level with each other, which would have meant that a horizontal line would cross two strips. I also made an effort to use a variety of tonal values and patterns and differing textures—laces, rough linens, smooth silks, and pebbled cottons—to give the finished garment added interest.

I give here, in a black-and-white graphic diagram, an arrangement of shapes and tonal values showing how they appeared in the back of the sixteenth-century dofuko responsible for the birth of this book. You need not follow this plan. It is shown only to provide a jumping-off point for those not yet brave enough to design their own "abstract painting" patchwork.

It is best to start this kind of patching on the left, where column A stands in the diagram. Column B is arranged to build on column A. Column C then builds on the abstract foundation already created by the juxtaposition of the first two columns.

For patching in the Japanese sixteenth-century manner, cut or tear various fabrics in strips 7 inches in width. (For making the same kind of patchwork on a more refined scale, simply cut narrower strips.) As you will note, some of the patches are narrow vertical strips sewn together to equal the width of the 7-inch-wide strip. Cut or tear these narrow strips 4 inches wide.

When cutting two patches to be sewn together by a diagonal seam, lay them end to end and right side up on the table (see diagram). Move strip A over strip B. Use a ruler and a light or dark coloring pencil, whichever is more visible on the fabric, and draw a diagonal line across the overlapped pieces. Cut along this line, cutting both pieces of fabric at the same time. Remove

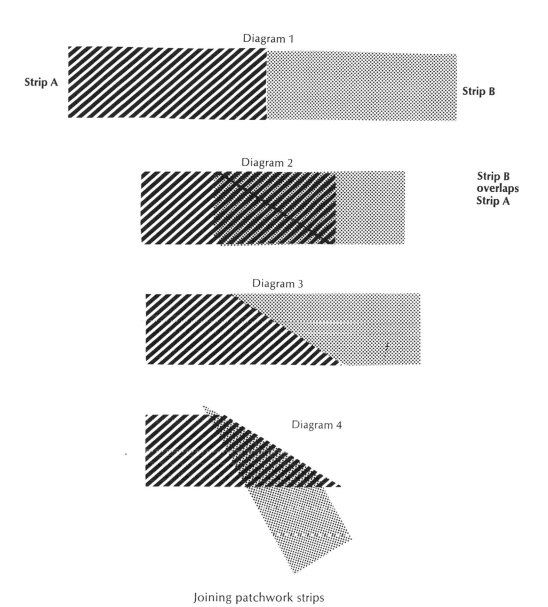

Diagram 1

Strip A

Strip B

Diagram 2

Strip B
overlaps
Strip A

Diagram 3

Diagram 4

Joining patchwork strips

the small unwanted pieces of strips *A* and *B* (see diagram 3). Lay fabric *B* face down over fabric *A*, as shown in diagram 4. Pin along the matching diagonal edges. Give a ½-inch seam allowance. Sew the two patches together, then *press the seam open*. The joined pieces will look like diagram 3.

The 7-inch width of the raw-edged strips allows for trimming to a 6-inch width. The clean-cut 6-inch strips will be seamed together lengthwise with a ½-inch seam allowance on each side. Once a part of the patchwork, each finished strip will measure 5 inches in width.

As I mentioned above, if you want a more refined scale of patchwork, cut narrower strips. Simply remember to add 2 inches to the width you want your finished strips to be in the patchwork, so as to allow 1 inch for trimming, and two ½-inch seams.

Before the long strips are sewn together lengthwise, they must be trimmed. To help you do this neatly and easily, draw two lines on your muslin-covered work surface. Draw them parallel to the front edge of the table. Draw the first line 6½ inches from the edge and the second line 6 inches from the edge.

Lay the untrimmed 7-inch-wide strip *face down* along the front edge of your work area so that one side of the strip lies along the line 6½ inches away from the table edge, and the other side of the strip extends over the edge of the table. Trim this excess away. Your scissors will cut a very clean line if the blades are kept in front of and parallel to the edge of your table. The blades open and close freely but the edge of the table acts as a cutting guide.

After trimming one side of the patchwork strip, turn it around and lay it, still face down, so that its already trimmed side lies along the second line drawn on your table, the line 6 inches from the edge. Trim away the excess ½ inch on the side of the strip that extends over the table's edge. The trimmed strip will measure exactly 6 inches in width.

When you are ready to sew two strips together with a lengthwise seam, lay one strip face up on the table. Lay a second strip face down on top of the first strip. Pin along the side where you will sew the seam. Put the pins in at right angles to the seam line. Make sure to *keep open* all seams crossing each strip. After machine stitching the lengthwise seam, remove the pins and press the long seam open.

Sew each succeeding row to the one preceding it in the manner described above.

Make each piece of patchwork a bit longer and wider than the muslin pattern piece you will use when cutting the patchwork into its final shape for use in making a garment. *Do not cut the patchwork yet.*

Before cutting the patchwork, mount it on a piece of lawn or voile, following the instructions given on page 17, or quilt it, following the instructions given on page 18. Only after the patchwork has been fully prepared—that is, either mounted or quilted—should you lay a muslin pattern piece over it and cut it into its final shape, ready to become part of a garment.

Patchwork strips
sewn together

JAPANESE "SAMPLER" PATCHWORK

This is so named because it was designed to look like a pattern found in a Japanese needlework sampler.

This patchwork is made of narrow vertical strips of unpatched fabric sewn between wider vertical strips of patches.

Cut or tear narrow vertical strips 2 inches in width. Cut the patchwork pieces for this kind of design *exactly* the right size and shape. I give here an outline of the cutting guide I used for the Japanese sampler patchwork jacket illustrated in Plate 9. Use sandpaper for making the template for cutting your patches.

Make two kinds of patched rectangles, one having a single diagonal band across its center, the other having three diagonal bands across its center. Sew these rectangles together in vertical rows as shown in the diagram. *Press all seams open*. Trim the strips. Sew strip A to a narrow strip, A_1. Sew strip B to strip A_1, as shown in the diagram. Sew narrow strip B_1 to strip B, as shown, and continue in this fashion until the patchwork is large enough for the pattern piece you will cut from it.

Japanese "sampler" patchwork

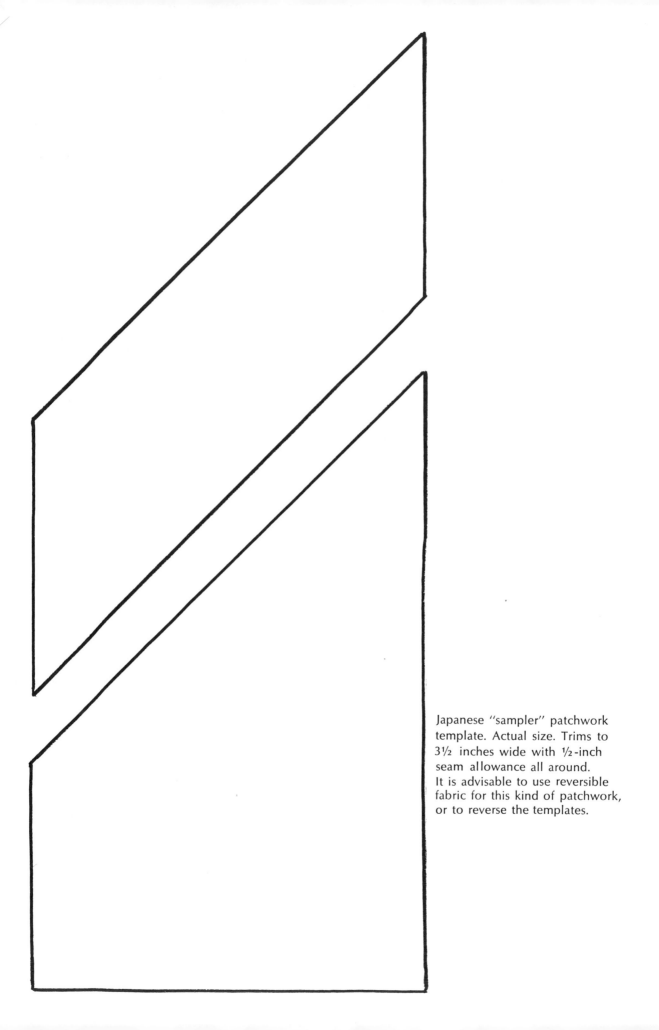

Japanese "sampler" patchwork
template. Actual size. Trims to
3½ inches wide with ½-inch
seam allowance all around.
It is advisable to use reversible
fabric for this kind of patchwork,
or to reverse the templates.

IMARI,
OR TORTOISESHELL
PATCHWORK

This is *not* made of hexagon-shaped patches, but of half-hexagon patches sewn in vertical strips. When the strips are seamed together, the fabrics, if properly placed, result in hexagons with vertical center seams.

In this type of patchwork it is *very* important to cut patches of exactly the right shape. I give here an outline for the template to use. It is the same size as the one used in the Imari patchwork illustrated in Plates 12, 13, and 14.

Use sandpaper for making the template for the half-hexagon patches.

Arrange piles of patches in the kind of repeat pattern you want to use. Make a vertical strip like the one shown in column *A*. Use ½-inch seams to join the patchwork pieces. Press the seams open. Make a second vertical strip of patches as shown in column *B*. Press the seams open. Then with right sides facing each other, pin the strips together. Sew the vertical seam. Press the seam open. Make a third strip, as shown in column *C*. Sew it to strip *B*. Continue patching in this fashion until your patchwork is big enough for the pattern piece you will cut from it.

Imari or tortoiseshell patchwork template. Actual size. The ½-inch seam allowance is marked all around.

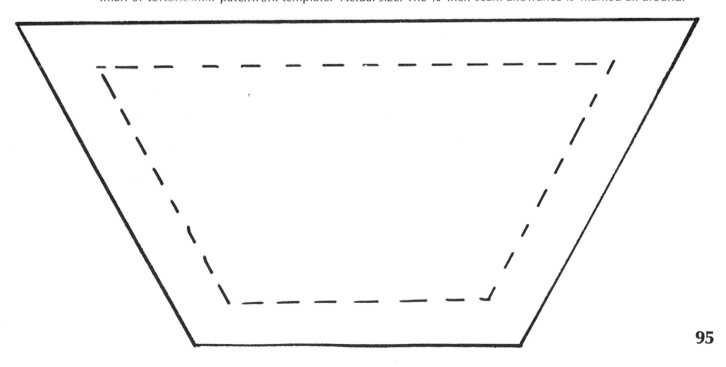

Imari or tortoiseshell patchwork

ARROWHEAD
PATCHWORK

This is made with vertical strips of parallelogram patches. Use sandpaper for making your template for the patches. A suggested shape for you to use is given here, with measurements, but reduced in size for lack of space on the page.

Make vertical strips and sew them together as shown in the diagram, or as shown in the black, brown, and gray winter coat with the tiny gray knots on it (Plate 5) or in the variation in Plate 15.

Press all seams open.

Arrowhead patchwork template. Enlarge to 13 inches long and 4 inches wide.

Arrowhead patchwork

FISH-SCALE
PATCHWORK

This is made of pieces of fabric cut into identical scallops. Use sandpaper for making the template for all the patches. See outline of actual size of scallop patch used in the fish-scale patchwork coats illustrated in this book (Plates 4 and 21).

Cut *yards* and *yards* of bias binding. Bind each scallop as shown in the outline. Turn the bias binding toward the back of the patch. It is not necessary to fold under the raw edges of the bias binding at the back of each patch. Simply baste the binding in place. With the front of the patch toward you, run your stitches along the original machine-stitched seam. Press.

Stack the finished patches of identical fabrics in piles. Arrange the piles in rows, creating the pattern you want to use and repeat in your patchwork.

Begin patching at the bottom.

Lay a row of bound scallops along the edge of your table. Lay the next row of scallops overlapping the first row, as shown in the diagram. Pin the two rows of scallops together. Baste, then machine stitch, following the basting stitches used to turn back the bias binding. After sewing each new row onto the preceding row, cut away the excess fabric in back, leaving only ¼ inch of fabric next to the machine-stitched seam.

When the piece of patchwork is finished, slip stitch the outer edge of each scale to the scales under it. This will make the patchwork lie flat and will make it easy to press.

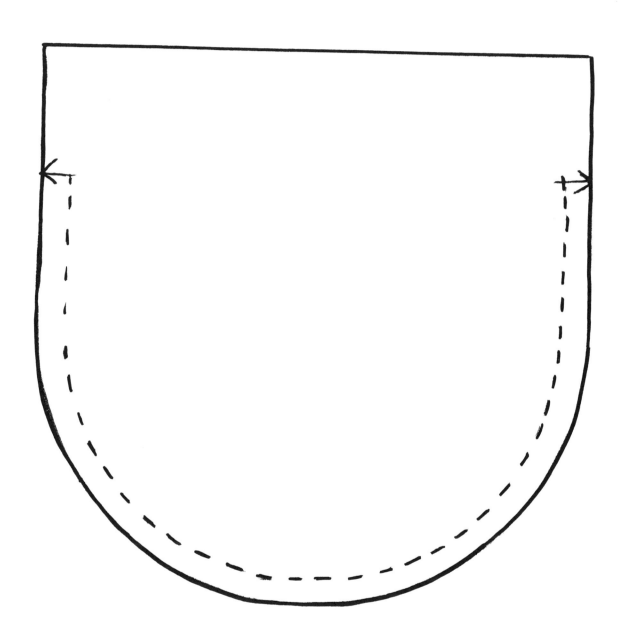

Fish-scale patchwork template. Actual size. Bias seam binding goes from arrow to arrow sewn along the dotted line.

Fish-scale patchwork

Postscript

A few remarks on the word *costume*, on my philosophy of color, of dressing, and of the use of accessories, and an additional thought or two follow here.

The Oxford Universal Dictionary defines the word *costume* as the fashion proper to the time and locality in which a *scene* is laid. *Costume* is also the mode of personal attire and dress belonging to a nation, a *class*, or a period. (The emphasis is mine.)

The word *costume* therefore means at least two things: the first meaning pertains to garments worn in a theatrical performance, the second to clothes signifying a person's level in society.

Every morning, each one of us dresses for the day, covering our bodies with clothes—in a sense these are our disguise—chosen from the costumes available to us. I find it sad that department stores offer such impersonal clothes, but at least we *do* have a choice. And whether or not we realize it, what we choose to wear reveals what we think about ourselves, for we are dressing ourselves for our part in the play—where "all the world's a stage."

I had wanted to use the word *costume* in the title of this book, but was dissuaded: the theatrical implications in the word might be misleading, "they" said. However, "they" didn't know how I feel about clothes. And so here, tucked away in the back of the book where "they" may never see it, I will use the word freely, because its double meaning, both theatrical and social, defines exactly the purpose these patterns are meant to serve; they should offer us a way to clothe our bodies in a most personal manner, in the costume of our choice for the part we have selected to play in life, thereby telling the world *who* we really are, and *where* we stand in society.

A costume is not complete without accessories. The clothes in this book, being as simply cut as they are, present the perfect foil for jewels—like plots and subplots. Rings, bracelets, necklaces, and earrings in many colors should belong to every person owning any patchwork attire. For this reason I have included in this book the two photographs of necklaces and earrings I have collected to wear with my own patchwork costumes (Plates 23 and 24).

Lately I have become even more fascinated with jewelry. I do not own or wear much of it that is valuable in the sense of being made with precious stones. I prefer to collect semiprecious pendants—which I have recently learned to incorporate into necklaces that I knot and string for myself. The personal choice that we all should have is here again available to us if we make our own accessories.

Since I began stringing my own necklaces I have learned that the saying "less is more" indeed applies here. The tie rack on the inside of my closet door where I hang my long necklaces to keep them from tangling used to be stocked with ropes of many colors, each of closely knotted beads. But I began to sense that with the simpler clothes I had begun to wear, the weighty look of such dense necklaces was too heavy for the gracious elegance I wished to affect in my costumes. The few good Chinese necklaces I owned were the ones I found myself choosing more and more often to wear with my soft, easy bias blouses and untailored Indian pants. The obvious step to take next: restring my collection of beads, using fewer for each necklace, spacing them out on silken cords, giving each bead more air in which to breathe, and thereby making it look *far* more precious! (See Plate 23.)

By the same token, earrings that hang from the ear and move a little look so much more alive and enticing than heavy, unmoving studs attached to the ear lobe. So now I own a pair of curved gold wires for my pierced ears. On these two small, hardly visible supports I hang, every morning, a pair of little pendant beads to match the necklace I have chosen to wear that day. I find the system perfect because on my one pair of gold wires I can hang any bead my jeweler prepares with the little peg and loop. He takes a gold wire with a pinhead on it, runs the wire through the bead, and makes a secure loop on the other side with what he calls a "pigtail" twist. The loop slips on my gold wire, and the bead hangs free! (See Plate 24.)

The clothes I choose to wear now follow and express my philosophy of color in which every hue is a note in a musical scale. A single tone may be lovely in itself if its timbre—or aural texture—has an interesting and attractive quality. (The oboe comes to mind.) Two tones sounded together begin to make a chord. But three really satisfy the ear. So it is with color.

Most often I choose a blouse of one color, a pair of Indian pants of another, and top it off with a coat of unquilted patchwork combining the two colors and including a third or even a fourth note. Or I may wear only two colors in the costume but add the third, the sharpest color, when I choose the necklace, earrings, handbag, and shoes to complete the costume.

And now each day begins with pleasant and deliberate thoughts about how to dress most effectively for the part I will play.

So go ahead. Have fun with this book. Give yourself a wardrobe of very personal costumes, vibrant with color, rich in texture, and full of warmth, all qualities guaranteed to make unique the part you choose to play.

103

Bibliography

Bishop, Edna Bryte, and Arch, Marjorie Statler. *The Bishop Method of Clothing Construction*. New York: J. B. Lippincott Company, 1966.

Minnich, Helen Benton. *Japanese Costume*. Rutland, Vermont, and Tokyo: Charles E. Tuttle, 1963.

Noma, Seiroko. *Japanese Costume and Textile Arts*. New York: Weatherhill; Tokyo: Heibonsha, 1974.

Shaver, Ruth M. *Kabuki Costume*. Rutland, Vermont, and Tokyo: Charles E. Tuttle, 1966.

Textile Designs of Japan. 2 volumes. Osaka, Japan: Japan Textile Color Design Center, 1959–60.

Wilcox, R. Turner. *The Dictionary of Costume*. New York: Charles Scribner's Sons, 1969.

Wilcox, R. Turner. *Folk and Festival Costume of the World*. New York: Charles Scribner's Sons, 1965.